Remembering
the Reformation

The Pro Ecclesia Series

Books in The Pro Ecclesia Series are "for the Church." The series is sponsored by the Center for Catholic and Evangelical Theology, founded by Carl Braaten and Robert Jenson in 1991. The series seeks to nourish the Church's faithfulness to the gospel of Jesus Christ through a theology that is self-critically committed to the biblical, dogmatic, liturgical, and ethical traditions that form the foundation for a fruitful ecumenical theology. The series reflects a commitment to the classical tradition of the Church as providing the resources critically needed by the various churches as they face modern and post-modern challenges. The series will include books by individuals as well as collections of essays by individuals and groups. The Editorial Board will be drawn from various Christian traditions.

OTHER TITLES IN THE SERIES INCLUDE:

- *The Morally Divided Body: Ethical Disagreement and the Disunity of the Church*, edited by Michael Root and James J. Buckley

- *Christian Theology and Islam*, edited by Michael Root and James J. Buckley

- *Who Do You Say That I Am? Proclaiming and Following Jesus Today*, edited by Michael Root and James J. Buckley

- *What Does It Mean to "Do This"? Supper, Mass, Eucharist*, edited by Michael Root and James J. Buckley

- *Heaven, Hell, . . . and Purgatory?*, edited by Michael Root and James J. Buckley

- *Life Amid the Principalities: Identifying, Understanding, and Engaging Created, Fallen, and Disarmed Powers Today*, edited by Michael Root and James J. Buckley

Remembering
the Reformation

Commemorate? Celebrate? Repent?

Edited by

Michael Root &
James J. Buckley

CASCADE *Books* · Eugene, Oregon

REMEMBERING THE REFORMATION
Commemorate? Celebrate? Repent?

Pro Ecclesia Series 7

Cascade Books
An Imprint of Wipf and Stock Publishers
199 W. 8th Ave., Suite 3
Eugene, OR 97401

www.wipfandstock.com

PAPERBACK ISBN: 978-1-5326-1668-6
HARDCOVER ISBN: 978-1-4982-4060-4
EBOOK ISBN: 978-1-4982-4059-8

Cataloguing-in-Publication data:

Names: Root, Michael, 1951–, editor. | Buckley, James J., 1947–, editor.

Title: Remembering the reformation : commemorate? celebrate? repent? / edited by Michael Root and James J. Buckley.

Description: Eugene, OR : Cascade Books, 2017 | Pro Ecclesia Series 7

Identifiers: ISBN 978-1-5326-1668-6 (paperback) | ISBN 978-1-4982-4060-4 (hardcover) | ISBN 978-1-4982-4059-8 (ebook)

Subjects: LCSH: Reformation. | Protestantism. | Reformation—Anniversaries, etc.

Classification: BR309 .R38 2017 (paperback) | BR309 .R38 (ebook)

Manufactured in the U.S.A.   12/05/17

Contents

Contributors

James J. Buckley is Professor of Theology at Loyola University Maryland. He is a member of the North American Lutheran Catholic dialogue. He and Frederick Christian Bauerschmidt recently published *Catholic Theology: An Introduction* (Wiley Blackwell, 2017).

Thomas FitzGerald is Professor of Church History and Historical Theology at Holy Cross Greek Orthodox School of Theology in Brookline, Massachusetts. He is the Orthodox Executive Secretary of the Orthodox-Catholic Theological Consultation in North America. He represented the Ecumenical Patriarchate on the senior staff of the World Council of Churches in Geneva, Switzerland, from 1994 to 2000. His publications include *The Ecumenical Movement* (Greenwood, 2004), *The Orthodox Church* (Greenwood, 1995), and *The Ecumenical Patriarchate and Christian Unity* (Holy Cross Press, 1997, 2009). With his wife, Dr. Kyriaki FitzGerald, he is coauthor of *Living the Beatitudes: Perspectives from Orthodox Spirituality* (Holy Cross Press, 2000, 2006).

Stanley Hauerwas is the Gilbert T. Rowe Professor Emeritus of Divinity and Law at Duke University. He is retired but still working, because that is what bricklayers do. Before retirement he published more than forty books in the field of theology and ethics. His writings cover a wide range of subjects, including political theology, philosophical theology, ecclesiology, medical ethics, and issues concerning the care of the dying and those living with mental illness and disabilities. He is credited for being a leading figure in recovering virtue theory. In 2001 *Time* named him "Best Theologian in America," to which he responded, "'Best' is not a theological category."

Sarah Hinlicky Wilson is an Adjunct Professor of the Institute for Ecumenical Research in Strasbourg, France; the editor of the independent theological quarterly *Lutheran Forum*; and an ordained pastor in the Evangelical Lutheran Church in America. She has lectured on topics in Lutheran and ecumenical theology in Ethiopia, Madagascar, Taiwan, and throughout Europe and the United States. She is the author of more than a hundred articles on theological topics as well as two books: *Woman, Women, and the Priesthood in the Trinitarian Theology of Elisabeth Behr-Sigel* (2013), and *A Guide to Pentecostal Movements for Lutherans* (2016). She makes her home in Saint Paul, Minnesota, with her husband, Andrew, and son, Ezekiel.

Bishop Charles Morerod, OP is Bishop of Lausanne, Geneva, and Fribourg, and author of *Ecumenism and Philosophy: Philosophical Questions for a Renewal of Dialogue*, trans. Therese C. Scarpelli (Sapientia Press, 2006). Formerly Professor of Theology and Philosophy at the Pontifical University of St. Thomas Aquinas (Rome) and Secretary General of the International Theological Commission.

Michael Root is Professor of Systematic Theology at The Catholic University of America. He was formerly the Director of the Institute for Ecumenical Research, Strasbourg, France.

Preface

IN 1517, MARTIN LUTHER set off what has been called, at least since the nineteenth century, the Protestant Reformation. Can Christians of differing traditions commemorate the upcoming 500th anniversary of this event together? How do we understand and assess the Reformation today? What calls for celebration? What calls for repentance? Can the Reformation anniversary be an occasion for greater mutual understanding among Catholics, Orthodox, and Protestants? At the 2015 Pro Ecclesia annual conference for clergy and laity, meeting at the Catholic University of America in Washington, DC, Catholic and Orthodox, Evangelical Lutheran and American Evangelical, as well as Methodist, scholars addressed this topic. The aim of this book is not only to collect together these diverse Catholic and Evangelical perspectives but also to provide resources for all Christians, including pastors and scholars, to think and argue about the roads we have taken since 1517—as we also learn to pray with Jesus Christ "that all may be one" (John 17:21).

Michael Root's opening reflection focuses on the events of 1517, and how past polemics between Catholics and Protestants have been largely replaced by consensus on the details immediately before and after Luther's theses. However, there are also ongoing arguments over how the Reformation fits into the larger story of a de-Christianized Western civilization—arguments in which Catholics disagree with Catholics and Evangelicals with Evangelicals as much or more than Catholics and Evangelicals disagree with each other. This suggests that, while a differentiated consensus on the events before and after 1517 is a necessary condition of Catholic and Evangelical engagement, it is not a sufficient condition. Our other authors raise some of these other issues.

Stanley Hauerwas offers an account, at once personal and tuned to the diverse communities that constitute "the Reformation," that seeks a post-Constantinan way to do ethics together. Catholic Bishop Charles Morerod proposes that the tragedy of the Reformation, with persons on both sides to blame, needs to face the way that theological questions must face philosophical disagreements between Catholics and Evangelicals over divine and human action to advance the conversation. Evangelical Lutheran Sarah Hinlicky Wilson proposes that this first commemoration of the Reformation in an ecumenical age must commemorate and repent before celebrating the Reformation—all under a Gospel that calls us to recognize that "we are beggars all." Thomas FitzGerald reminds us that, along with the deepening divide between the Church of Rome and the Orthodox in the sixteenth century, there were interactions between some Orthodox and Catholics and Protestants from which we can learn even as we can go further. Michael Root outlines a number of practical challenges to commemorating the Reformation and proposes a new way to think about Christian ecumenism in view of current impasses of Church and ministry, including ordination of women and gays.

In conclusion, we have included a final page of resources for continuing the discussion of commemorating, repenting, and/or celebrating the Reformation. Some events have already occurred in 2016 as steps toward the 2017 commemorations (e.g., Pope Francis's commemoration in Sweden in the fall 2016). And the issues raised by these commemorations will certainly extend well beyond 2017. We hope that this volume in the *Pro Ecclesia* series, like the other volumes, is a resource for pastors and theologians and all Christians to journey together as Catholics and Evangelicals.

Michael Root, Catholic University of America
James J. Buckley, Loyola University Maryland

1

1517: What Are We Commemorating?[1]

Michael Root

TWO THOUSAND SEVENTEEN WILL be a year of significant historical and ecumenical commemoration, but just what are we commemorating? What in fact happened? Can Catholics and Protestants answer that question together in agreed detail? In this essay, I will address these two questions. First, what happened? And second, can Catholics and Protestants give a shared description of those events?

From the start, historical accounts of the Reformation tended to be polemical. Neither side in the sixteenth century debates accepted that the other was acting in good, if erroneous, faith. Catholic accounts of the Reformation were often attacks on Luther's personality. The Catholic Heinrich Denifle's 1904 study of Luther included such chapter titles as "The Duping of Nuns by Luther," "Luther's Sophisms and Distortions," and "Luther's Buffoonery."[2] And Denifle was not a crude polemicist without regard for history, but a prominent and well-respected medieval historian, who conducted extensive archival research (it was Denifle who found Luther's early

1. This essay began as an oral presentation and preserves some aspects of its oral form. Footnotes are not as detailed as a more formal paper would demand.

2. Heinrich Denifle, *Luther and Lutherdom, from Original Sources*, trans. Raymund Volz (Somerset, OH: Torch, 1917).

Romans lectures in the Vatican Archive) and was on his way to Cambridge to receive an honorary doctorate when he died in 1905.

Protestant historians often placed Luther and the Reformation in the opposite light. In the nineteenth century, the German Protestant Leopold Ranke insisted that history is not about fables, but about "what really happened," *was eigentlich geschehen ist*, but in his *History of the Reformation in Germany*, he opens his account of the events of the Reformation with the statement: "Was not the Gospel itself kept concealed by the Roman church? . . . It was necessary to clear the germ of religion from the thousand folds of accidental forms under which it lay concealed, and to place it unencumbered in the light of day," which task, in Ranke's view, the Reformation accomplished.[3] Even in the mid-twentieth century popular biography of Luther, Roland Bainton's *Here I Stand*, a book assigned to me in college, there can be no doubt who are the good guys and the bad guys.[4]

The last fifty years have seen important changes. Historians without a confessional axe to grind have become deeply involved in Reformation history. In the 1930s a school of Catholic Reformation scholarship developed which, while clearly Catholic in various ways, opened up a much better picture of the Catholic reaction to Luther, investigated without prejudice the problems of the late-medieval church, and recognized what, by Catholic standards also, was an authentic evangelical core to Luther's teaching. Protestant scholars appropriated and added to the new work by non-confessional and Catholic scholars. Polemical or hagiographical accounts are still to be found (and new ones will undoubtedly be written in the next few years), but we now can speak of a common, ecumenical exploration of what are rightly called the Reformations of the sixteenth century, reformations that left no strand of Western Christianity unchanged.

A task for all of us in the lead-up to the 2017 events should be some engagement with this historical work. The international Catholic-Lutheran dialogue has put together a solid summary in its recent text *From Conflict to Communion*. Here one can find both an account of the most important events of the Reformation and a summary of the most important aspects of Luther's theology, put together by a team of Lutheran and Catholic scholars. That such a text could be written is itself a sign that times have changed.

---

3. Leopold von Ranke, *History of the Reformation in Germany*, trans. Sarah Austin (New York: F. Unger, 1966) 1, 121.

4. Roland Herbert Bainton, *Here I Stand: A Life of Martin Luther* (London: Hodder and Stoughton, 1951).

If one is interested in the larger history of the Reformation, in its political and cultural as well as its theological and ecclesial aspects, I would heartily recommend Diarmaid MacCulloch's *The Reformation*.[5] MacCulloch is somewhat weak on theology, but he tells a lively story which summarizes recent studies and includes a full picture of the Reformation beyond the usual focus on Luther and Calvin, especially highlighting the reforms that had begun prior to Luther in areas that remained Catholic, e.g., Spain and Italy. MacCulloch packs a great deal of learning into what reads almost like a take-to-the-beach book. An eminently readable and quite brief introduction to Luther and his theology can be found in Scott Hendrix's *Martin Luther: A Very Short Introduction*, which includes an extensive bibliography for those who want to read further.[6]

All of this is not to say that all historical disputes have disappeared in a puff of consensus. Some questions of fact remain unsettled and, unless new documents are found, are probably unanswerable. At least for the popular mind, the most prominent such question is whether Luther did or did not actually nail the 95 Theses on the Power of Indulgences to the door of the Castle Church on October 31, 1517. The earliest account that he did so comes from the early 1540s, twenty-five years after the event. We have no statement from Luther or from any eyewitness that he did so. Evidence can be cited that would lead one to think he did or that he didn't. Scholars still disagree on the question, although we know for certain that he wrote a letter to Archbishop Albrecht of Magdeburg, protesting the indulgence campaign, on October 31st and that Luther himself later cited October 31st as the day on which his protest had begun.[7]

Apart from a few such details, however, we have a fairly good picture of who did and said what when in the Reformation. Historians today paint a far more variegated picture of the Reformation than was the case even fifty years ago. I will here go on using the term "the Reformation," but the question must be asked whether there was such a singular phenomenon. Carter Lindberg titled his recent textbook *The European Reformations*, in the plural, distinguishing not only the different strands of Protestant reformation,

5. Diarmaid MacCulloch, *The Reformation* (New York: Viking, 2003).

6. Scott H. Hendrix, *Martin Luther: A Very Short Introduction* (Oxford: Oxford University Press, 2010).

7. For a survey of recent scholarship on this question, see Volker Leppin, "31. Oktober 1517—Der symbolische Anfang der Reformation und die lutherische Festkultur," in *Tage der Revolution—Feste der Nation*, ed. Rolf Gröschner and Wolfgang Reinhard (Tübingen: Mohr Siebeck, 2010) 55–72.

but also the thoroughgoing reform that took place in Catholicism.[8] We also today have a much richer picture of what the Reformation meant for art, family, politics, and economics. (A strength of the MacCulloch volume I mentioned is bringing out these wider aspects of the Reformation.)

The present historical problem in a sense comes from this richness. How do we fit it all together into a single coherent picture? Reformation studies has itself become a field that is difficult to grasp as a whole. Arguments are not, however, confessional. The various sides in scholarly debates today cannot be identified as Catholic, Lutheran, Reformed, or Anglican. Nevertheless, one's larger theological judgments do make some difference when one moves from readily describable, even if complex, events to assessment. Was the Reformation a triumph or a tragedy? And if in some sense both, in just what sense both? Was division the virtually inevitable result of an evangelical theology that was at its basis incompatible with any recognizable form of what Western Catholicism had become, or was reconciliation a possibility for years and even decades after 1517? If so, what blocked reconciliation? Blame is certainly shared by all sides, but blame for what? Theological blindness? Financial or political self-interest? Personal stubbornness or vainglory?

These are the questions of historical assessment that need to be addressed as part of the commemoration of the beginning of the Reformation. Let me focus for most of the rest of this presentation on what we can agree occurred at the Reformation's beginning, the events unleashed by Luther's protest of October 31, 1517, whether that protest was nailed, or merely mailed. I use the word "unleashed" deliberately, for a certain mismatch of action and effect occurs. An unknown professor of theology at an undistinguished university circulates some theses for debate to his colleagues and sends them also with a cover letter to one or more bishops—and the unity of Western Christendom collapses. Now, I have always thought very highly of the world-historical importance of the ideas put forward by theology professors, but something here calls for explanation. How did such a small, even trivial occurrence have such consequences? Obviously, more was going on than meets the eye. Somehow, Luther's protest was like a snowball at the top of a snow-covered slope, which, rolling down the slope, sets off an avalanche.

At the end of this essay, I give a detailed chronology of the events stretching from October 1517 through early 1519 (at which point, a brief

8. Carter Lindberg, *The European Reformations* (Oxford: Blackwell, 1996).

pause occurred in developments). During those sixteen or so months, events happened quickly, especially in light of the uncertain and often slow communications of the time. Behind the events stand two trajectories which came into decisive collision.

On the one hand, the evolution of indulgences had reached an inflationary stage in Luther's time.[9] Indulgences—technically put, the remission of the penitential satisfactions that must be completed even for forgiven sins—had a complex history about which research over the last century has laid much bare. Indulgences were not a static reality in the medieval church, but had undergone significant evolution, and were evolving further in the early sixteenth century. From a limited and extraordinary concession in the early High Middle Ages, associated with the Crusades and Jubilee Years in Rome, they had undergone two major expansions. During the Great Schism of the late fourteenth century, one of the competing popes, Boniface IX, extended indulgences associated with certain sites or shrines (for example, the Portiuncula indulgence associated with St. Francis's church in Assisi) to chosen churches throughout Europe (or at least those parts of Europe that recognized his papacy). A cross and the papal coat of arms would be erected in a local church and a visit to that church on certain days would gain the same indulgence as, say, a pilgrimage to Rome during a Jubilee Year. Indulgences thus became far more available to a wide swath of European Christians.

More importantly, in 1476 an even greater expansion occurred. Pope Sixtus IV, in a bull declaring an indulgence associated with a church in France, explicitly stated that an indulgence acquired could be applied to the dead in purgatory. This view had been put forward by various persons earlier, but had not received official approbation prior to 1476. In addition, the bishop associated with this particular church in France, Cardinal

9. The following history of the development of indulgences in the years just prior to 1517 is heavily dependent on Bernd Moeller, "Die letzten Ablasskampagnen: Der Widerspruch Luthers gegen den Ablass in seinem geschichtlichen Zusammenhang," in *Lebenslehren und Weltentwürfe im Übergang vom Mittelalter zur Neuzeit: Politik, Bildung, Naturkunde, Theologie: Bericht über Kolloquien der Kommission zur Erforschung der Kultur des Spätmittelalters, 1983 bis 1987*, ed. Harmut Boockmann, Karl Stackmann, and Bernd Moeller (Göttingen: Vandenhoeck & Ruprecht, 1989) 539–67. For the earlier medieval history of indulgences, see Robert W. Shaffern, *The Penitent's Treasury: Indulgences in Latin Christianity 1175–1375* (Scranton: University of Scranton Press, 2007). For a brief ecumenical account of the theology of indulgences, see Michael Root, "Indulgences as Ecumenical Barometer: Penitence and Unity in the Christian Life." *Bulletin of the Centro Pro Unione (Rome)* 39 (2011) 3–9.

Raymund Peraudi, organized the promotion of the indulgence with the skill of a highly successful modern fundraiser. Peraudi was a true believer in indulgences as a wonderful outpouring of grace. They should be offered enthusiastically and dramatically. Peraudi became the master of the indulgence campaign, a series of sermons and liturgies carried out during a specified period in a particular territory, associated with good works for some cause, such as funding defense against the Ottomans or rebuilding a church. As had become common, among the good works that could be done to acquire the indulgence was a financial contribution, and this good work became the predominant form of good work associated with the indulgence. While it does not appear that Peraudi was himself driven by an interest in financial gain, his high-powered campaigns turned out to be lucrative (not, it should be noted, so much for the papacy, as for the local officials who always received a major portion of money donated). The turn of the sixteenth century saw an indulgence boom. In the fifteen years prior to 1517, seven major indulgence campaigns were carried out in Germany: to fund a crusade against schismatic Ruthenians; to rebuild the cathedral in Konstanz, the Dominican church in Augsburg, and a church in Brüx; to restore the cathedral in Trier; to repair dikes in the Netherlands; and, famously, to build a new St. Peter's in Rome, the indulgence campaign against which Luther protested. Scheduling and geographically limiting each campaign so it would not compete with others became a headache and there is some evidence that financial returns were beginning to diminish, stimulating even greater efforts. (It should be noted that Luther's protest was effective in this regard, that the St. Peter's indulgence campaign was the beginning of the end for such indulgence campaigns aimed at fundraising.)

These often crude campaigns highlighted an ambiguity that lay within indulgences. Indulgences were (and I would note still are) special events in which the faithful are called to acts of penance and self-reflection, with which the church as a whole, Christ and the saints, join in solidarity, offering their works in prayer for divine assistance in that penance. Indulgences were originally understood as an aid to penance, based on the reality that the penitent is not alone but is aided by his or her brothers and sisters in Christ, including Christ himself. In the indulgence campaigns of Luther's time, indulgences seem to have become not an aid to penance, but a substitute for penance. Inner penitence and the external act required for the indulgence had become separated; one could obtain an indulgence to be applied to someone in purgatory without oneself going to confession (an innovation criticized by some at the time). That the good work associated with the indulgence had become for most persons a financial contribution to a specific good cause made the matter seem all the more like a strictly external transaction unrelated to inner transformation.

This evolution of indulgences encountered a second reality in transition: the developing theology of Martin Luther, who in 1517 was an unknown, Augustinian canon (to be precise, not a monk). The modern reader can trace Luther's development through the manuscripts of his classroom lectures, first on the Psalms from 1513 to 1515, then on Romans from 1515 to 1516, and on Galatians from 1516 to 1517. We also have letters and a few sermons. The interpretation of the evolution of Luther's thought in this period is a matter of controversy. A good deal of ink was spilled in the mid-twentieth century over attempts to specify just when Luther made his "Reformation breakthrough" and left behind the medieval theology in which he had been schooled. My sense is most interpreters today have abandoned the idea there was some single moment of insight in which the scales suddenly fell from Luther's eyes. Rather, his ideas developed gradually, with stops and starts and occasional retreats.

How to read this development will always, I think, be a matter of dispute, for any reading is also an interpretation of Luther's theology, a judgment about what were its central points and inner logic.[10] I think most would agree that during the period from 1515 through 1517, Luther had developed an outlook that focused intensely on inner penitence and humility. Any righteousness of one's own works, even works aided by grace, will always be radically inadequate before the judgment of God. The Christian can, however, be penitent, condemning his or her own sins. In the process, one aligns oneself with the righteousness of God and is, in an odd sense, by penitent self-condemnation, righteous. Thus, in his Romans lectures, Luther can refer to "total humility both against God and against man, that is, complete and perfect righteousness"[11] and can say "the only complete righteousness is humility."[12]

Especially for Luther in 1517, the Christian life was about penitence. Thus, the famous first thesis of the 95: "When our Lord and Master Jesus

10. The best recent study of this development is Berndt Hamm, *The Early Luther: Stages in a Reformation Reorientation*, trans. Martin J. Lohrmann (Grand Rapids: Eerdmans, 2014).

11. Martin Luther, *Lectures on Romans: Glosses and Scholia*, ed. Hilton C. Oswald, Luther's Works 25 (St. Louis: Concordia, 1972) 183.

12. Martin Luther, *Romans*, 441.

Christ said, 'Repent,' he willed the entire life of believers to be one of repentance."[13] Penitence is not a burden the Christian should seek to escape; it is our participation in the cross of Christ, the medicine of salvation. "A Christian who is truly contrite seeks and loves to pay penalties for his sins."[14] One can see why a theology and practice of indulgences in which as external a work as a financial contribution can substitute for true works of penitence would be more than a mere abuse for Luther; it would cut the heart out of the Christian life. Luther did not understand his protest against indulgences as parallel to, say, a criticism of the venality or immorality of the Renaissance papacy. His was a theological protest and for him the gospel was at stake.

The origin of Luther's protest lies thus in this collision between developments in the theology and practices of indulgences in the late fifteenth and early sixteenth centuries and the particular stamp of Luther's theology at the time. But we still have our question: how can this have set off an event as large as the Reformation? Much of Luther's critique of indulgences can be found throughout the late Middle Ages (though generally as a criticism of the multiplication of indulgences, rather than of indulgences themselves). The saying "repentance is better than indulgence" can be found among various late medieval authors.

Luther was never one to stay rigorously on topic, however, and the 95 Theses also contain various statements about the limitations of papal power in relation to purgatory and comments on the nature of confession and absolution. If Luther were only concerned with indulgences, then the entire discussion might have been a minor episode in the history of a minor aspect of Christian life. But the concern with indulgences was a manifestation of Luther's larger engagement with the topics that would be at the center of the Reformation: the nature of authority in the Church and the nature of the Christian's salvation. What at the beginning was an academic debate about indulgences was on the way to becoming the wider movement we call the Reformation. Let me make six comments about this history.

First, while the 95 Theses might seem to us dense and academic, they excited great interest. We know of four printings that occurred by the end of 1517, from Leipzig in the east to Basel in the west. Most of these printings

13. Martin Luther, "Ninety-Five Theses or Disputation on the Power and Efficacy of Indulgences," in vol. 31 of *Luther's Works*, ed. Harold J. Grimm (Philadelphia: Fortress, 1957) 25.

14. Ibid., 29.

occurred at the initiative of others, not Luther. The theses were translated into German and thus reached a much wider lay audience.

Second, the public Catholic response, which began in January 1518, focused less on indulgences themselves than on papacy and authority. Luther knew of papal statements on indulgences, but he understood them to be exhortations for the faithful to receive the indulgences, not normative teaching about indulgences and thus, by the standards of the time, not dogmatically binding. He insisted he was debating a doctrinally open question. His opponents contended that the papal bulls were in fact doctrinally normative. As a result of this focus of his opponents, the emphasis in the debate quickly shifted away from indulgences themselves to questions of authority. A significant question of historical interpretation is whether the logic of Luther's theology implied from the start a radical criticism of Catholic structures of authority, a criticism that would inevitably have emerged as the argument proceeded, or whether Luther was forced in this direction by his critics, who, it should be noted, made claims for papal authority that were extreme for their time and go well beyond present Catholic teaching, e.g., that the pope stood above scripture. I would add that almost all commentators agree that, with an exception I will note in a moment, the Catholic cause was not well served by those who wrote against Luther in these first years. They fed Luther's emerging view that his opponents were knaves, fools, or, in many cases, both.

Third, already in March 1518, a decisive intervention occurred. Luther was taken under the protective wing of his prince, the Elector of Saxony, Frederick the Wise. When Luther was called to Heidelberg by his order, Frederick permitted him to go, but insisted that Luther be returned, blocking any action to hold him in custody for examination or punishment. Frederick was decisive later in 1518 in having Luther heard by a papal official in Germany rather than in Rome. The power of secular princes within the Church had expanded during the Great Schism and the conciliar controversy of the late fourteenth and fifteenth centuries, so that Frederick's action should perhaps not be seen as that unusual.[15] Nevertheless, it should be emphasized that Frederick's actions in 1518 both preserved and transformed the nascent Reformation. From this point on, the Reformation was

15. On the growth of the role of the princes in the churches in the late medieval period, see e.g., Wilhelm Maurer, "Erwägungen und Verhandlungen über die geistliche Jurisdiktion der Bischöfe vor und während des augsburger Reichstags von 1530," in *Die Kirche und ihr Recht: Gesammelte Aufsätze zum evangelischen Kirchenrecht*, ed. Gerhard Müller (Tübingen: J. C. B. Mohr [Paul Siebeck], 1976) 209–10.

entwined with political considerations and interests. Church and state were so interwoven in the Holy Roman Empire that any church reform movement had to engage political affairs. The alliance with supportive princes and town councils may have been a blessing, curse, or both, but it was almost certainly a condition of survival for the Reformation.

Fourth, it is difficult to deny there was a rush to judgment on the part of Roman authorities. Archbishop Albrecht, to whom Luther had sent the 95 Theses, forwarded them to Rome for investigation almost immediately. Already in February 1518, Pope Leo instructed the Augustinian order to have Luther silenced. When that attempt failed, an official investigation was opened in Rome in May 1518. The papal official most engaged in the investigation, Sylvester Prierias, Master of the Papal Palace, quickly published a text denouncing Luther as a heretic. Luther complained, rightly enough, that prosecutor, judge, and jury had spoken before he had been heard. Fatefully, in early August of 1518, the Holy Roman Emperor Maximilian complained to Rome that Luther's views were having noxious effects in Germany and their circulation needed to be stopped. [The issue here was not the 95 Theses, but an anonymous summary of a sermon by Luther on the limits of the Church's power of excommunication. That Luther's sermons were being summarized by hearers and widely distributed is a sign of the interest his critique had aroused.) In response to the imperial complaint, in mid-August 1518 a summary judgment was made in Rome, declaring Luther an open and pertinacious heretic. He was not to be given a hearing, but confronted with the judgment and given the choice of recanting or being condemned. This declaration was not made public, but rumors spread.

Luther's demand, from 1518 until his final condemnation by the Empire in 1521, was that his errors be shown from Scripture, right reason (or the Fathers). The rapid negative judgment, prior to such a hearing, was meant, in the view of those who made it, to nip a potential schismatic movement in the bud. In that intention, the rapid denunciation most obviously failed. Would events have turned out differently if matters had been handled with more deliberation? Here lies one of the tantalizing what-ifs of the Reformation.

The greatest possibility for such a what-if lies in the fifth aspect of this history I want to stress: the interview Luther had with Cardinal Cajetan in Augsburg on October 12–14, 1518. Cajetan was by far the best theologian engaged in the Catholic argument with Luther in these first years.

His commentary on Aquinas' *Summa theologiae* was of great historical importance. He was perhaps the most important scholastic theologian of his generation. Ironically, he was himself disturbed by inaccurate claims being made for indulgences and had written a memo on the subject in the fall of 1517, at about the same time as Luther must have been writing the 95 Theses.

At the Elector Frederick's request, Cajetan met with Luther and discussed the accusations against him. To do so, he got permission from Rome not to immediately enforce the summary judgment. The meeting with Luther centered on two topics: the authority of the papal statement that indulgences draw on the merit of Christ and the saints, and a new topic that had emerged in the summer of 1518, Luther's assertion that the forgiveness of sins in confession is effective only if the person forgiven is certain that he or she has been effectively forgiven.

The meeting with Cajetan was either the great missed opportunity to achieve reconciliation before the momentum toward division had become overwhelming, or the demonstration that authentic reconciliation was already impossible. Cajetan made a genuine effort to understand Luther. His personal memos on Luther's theology written at this time make fascinating reading.[16] Without doubt, he fit Luther's often paradoxical assertions into the framework of the scholastic theology of the time and thus tended to miss their point. Jared Wicks, the best contemporary commentator on this encounter, refers to "a tragic difference in the levels of discourse" between Luther and Cajetan.[17] Nevertheless, Cajetan wrote a memo at the time proposing a solution to the question of the certainty of salvation much like that of the *Joint Declaration on the Doctrine of Justification*.

By the end of the encounter, Cajetan made only one demand: that Luther accept the authority of the papal bull *Unigenitus* (1343) which described indulgences as distributing to penitents the merits of Christ and the saints (without, it should be noted, making any mention of the application of indulgences to those in purgatory). Luther did not believe he could make this concession. As he wrote a month later:

16. These texts are collected in Jared Wicks, ed. and trans., *Cajetan Responds: A Reader in Reformation Controversy* (Washington, DC: Catholic University of America Press, 1978).

17. Jared Wicks, "Roman Reactions to Luther: The First Year, 1518," in *Luther's Reform: Studies on Conversion and the Church*, Veröffentlichungen des Instituts für europäische Geschichte Mainz, Abteilung Religionsgeschichte 35 (Mainz: P. von Zabern, 1992) 176.

> It has long been believed that whatever the Roman church says, damns, or wants, all people must eventually say, damn, or want, and that no other reason need be given than that the Apostolic See and Roman church hold that opinion. . . . If that is what is involved in the revocation that is demanded of me, I foresee nothing else than that one revocation will be followed by another and so *ad infinitum*. For if I should answer one of [Cajetan's] statements with a skill equal to his, he would quickly conjure up against me another idol out of his imagination (for Thomistic theology is remarkably fertile in producing subtle distinctions, a veritable Proteus).[18]

As that quotation makes clear, Luther's trust was not high. The day after the interview, he learned of the rumors about the Roman summary judgment against him. On October 17 and 18, he wrote to Cajetan, offering a moratorium on writings on indulgences (if his opponents also were silent), but again refusing a revocation. He received no answer to these letters (why Cajetan did not respond, we do not know) and he left Augsburg on the night of October 20.

As noted, the discussion with Cajetan came to focus on the authority of the papal bull *Unigenitus*. At least some of the time, Luther argued that this bull was not in fact a binding teaching document. After Luther's departure, Cajetan moved to clarify the situation by drafting a new papal statement, *Cum postquam,* which would unambiguously be official teaching. Pope Leo X immediately proclaimed this statement on November 9, 1518. When Luther received this statement in early 1519, his dissent was now much more straightforward.

I have gone through this history in what I hope is not too boring detail because it will undoubtedly come up in the commemorations of the next few years. This is not a pretty story. It is important to remember that we know far more about what was occurring than anyone actually involved at the time. Those involved suffered from the ecclesiastical equivalent of the fog of war. On the one hand, the Catholic opponents based their understanding of Luther on only a few texts. Even Cajetan, who made the most conscientious effort of the opponents to collect and read Luther's published statements, did not have the lecture notes which now form so important a part of our understanding of Luther at this point in his career. Luther, on the other hand, did not know that Archbishop Albrecht and the Emperor had denounced him to Rome. He thought it had been Dominicans who had

18. Martin Luther, "The Proceedings at Augsburg," in vol. 31 of *Luther's Works,* ed. Harold J. Grimm (Philadelphia: Fortress, 1957) 276–77.

denounced him (both Prierias and Johann Tetzel, the indulgence preacher against whom Luther protested, were Dominicans). Part of Luther's suspicions of Cajetan were based on Cajetan's being a Dominican. He was being persecuted by a Thomist cabal, he thought, who did not respect Scripture and the Fathers. In addition, while Luther repeatedly insisted that the 95 Theses were statements meant to initiate debate, not assertions that he was personally committed to when he wrote them, they do not read that way and most definitely were not read that way at the time, either by their supporters or their opponents.

Early 1519 saw a pause in the public debate. At the end of this part of the story, lines of opposition had been clearly drawn. Ominously, the focus of the debate had expanded and shifted. Already in November 1518, Luther wrote that the dispute over indulgences was not that central. Questions of authority and the nature of salvation, questions that had already surfaced in the interview with Cajetan, were far more important. By early 1519, Luther's own theological development had reached the stage that almost all interpreters today agree that, whatever may have been true in October 1517, in 1519 he held a genuinely Lutheran understanding of justification, one significantly different from that of any medieval school. I think it also needs to be mentioned that in late 1518 Luther starts to describe the conflict with Rome in apocalyptic terms, as a conflict with Antichrist, and with Antichrist there is no compromise.

A sign of contemporary hope, perhaps, is that Protestants and Catholics can tell this story together. Whether Luther is hero or villain (or some complicated mix of the two), I think most historians and theologians would tell the story in pretty much the way I have described. The major point of interpretive dispute, as I have noted, is the degree to which reconciliation was a real possibility at this early stage. For the most part, that question turns on how one reads Luther's theology of this time. Did it already demand a radical break with the received tradition, or was that theology compatible with a reform of that tradition? The dispute on that point is not, however, a Catholic/Protestant argument. There are Protestants as well as Catholics on both sides of that question.

Let me close with two cautionary notes. First, in commemorations, too much emphasis should not be placed on these early events. They may have been historically important, but they do not constitute, I believe, present divisions. Catholics and Protestants could agree on the issues raised in the indulgence controversy and perhaps still be divided. A full understanding of what broke Humpty Dumpty might be fascinating, but it would not put Humpty Dumpty back together again.

Second, the location of the difference in how Catholics and Protestants tell this story is not so much at the detailed level I have presented today, but at the level of the larger narratives we tell about the last seven or eight hundred years of Christian history. The famous Reformation monument in Geneva, Switzerland, with large, imposing statues of Calvin and other worthies, has above it the motto: *Post tenebras lux*, after darkness light. That slogan implies a narrative: a period of benighted obscurantism was replaced by evangelical clarity. Few scholars would explicitly sign on to that narrative today, but it is striking how it lives on in new forms. Already in the Geneva monument itself, the Reformation is equated with the growth of freedom of conscience, a historically complex idea at best. The growing divergence between mainline Protestants and Catholics on some ethical questions presents a temptation to develop new forms of that story.

A mirror-image narrative can be found among some Catholics. At least since the early twentieth century, the narrative has been put forward that after the grand synthesis of Aquinas, a decline set in with the logic chopping of Scotus and the (alleged) semi-Pelagianism of Ockham, which obscured true Catholicism and thus made possible the deeper errors of the Reformation, which in turn destroyed the unity of Western Christendom and lead to the relativism, individualism, and secularism of the modern world, with all of their attendant troubles. One might call this the "Scotus to Stalin" line which has been repeated with vigor recently in Brad Gregory's book *The Unintended Reformation*.[19]

The last hundred years have seen the growth of a truly common scholarly enterprise of investigating and understanding what we now must see as the comprehensive reformations—Catholic, Lutheran, Reformed, Anabaptist, and otherwise—of the sixteenth century. The difficult question that remains is fitting that detailed account into our larger understanding of the course of modern Western history. We need to make sure that arguments over that larger understanding are also ecumenical.

[Note to typesetter: the chronology below is a supplement to the first chapter. Please treat it as a part or continuation of the chapter, rather than as a separate piece. —Jacob]

19. Brad S. Gregory, *The Unintended Reformation: How a Religious Revolution Secularized Society* (Cambridge: Harvard University Press, 2012).

A Chronology of the Beginning of the Reformation

A. Prehistory

November 10, 1483   Birth of Luther, Eisleben, Germany.

July 17, 1505   Luther joins Augustinian Hermits in Erfurt.

Summer 1511   Luther transferred to Wittenberg.

B. The Indulgence Controversy

1517

January 22   Johannes Tetzel commissioned to preach St Peter's indulgence in province of Magdeburg.

April 10   Tetzel preaches indulgence in Jüterbog, close to Wittenberg. (St. Peter's indulgence not preached in Electoral Saxony.) Many persons from Wittenberg attend.

Sometime in Spring   Luther preaches sermon criticizing pursuit of indulgences in contrast to embracing penance and the cross.

September   *Disputation against Scholastic Theology* held in Wittenberg; theses by Luther.

October 31   Luther writes letter criticizing indulgence campaign to Bishop Albrecht; letter sent that day or soon thereafter, along with 95 Theses on Indulgences and perhaps a Treatise on Indulgences; probably also wrote similarly to a few other bishops. Some days later, distributes copies of theses to some friends; might have posted theses on the Castle Church door. Theses translated into German and widely distributed by end of year. Disputation on theses never held.

November 17   Albrecht's diocesan officials open Luther's packet of material, forward it to Albrecht.

December 1	Albrecht asks faculty of University of Mainz for opinion on texts from Luther.
December 10	Albrecht again requests response from Mainz faculty.
December 13	Sometime prior to this date, Albrecht sends texts of Luther to Rome, requesting that they be investigated.
December 17	Mainz faculty sends report to Albrecht; Luther's teaching "contrary to common theological opinion."

1518

Early January	Albrecht's complaint received in Rome.
January 20	Tetzel presents theses attacking Luther's 95 Theses at Frankfurt an der Oder; when copies arrive in Wittenberg, seized by students from bookseller and publicly burned.
February 3	Pope Leo X instructs Vicar General of Augustinian Hermits to silence Luther, who has been spreading "new dogmas." Augustinians given four months to settle matter.
February 13	Luther submits his *Explanations of the 95 Theses* to his bishop, asking permission to publish it.
Early March	Luther informed by his Augustinian superior, Staupitz, that Vicar General has ordered discipline of Luther. Luther is to attend German meeting of order in Heidelberg in April and give account of basis for his arguments.
March 5	Luther writes friend C. Scheurl that he did not intend 95 Theses to be widely distributed and that he doubts some things there said.
Mid-March	Luther requests permission from Saxon Elector Frederick to absent himself from University so that he can go to Heidelberg. Frederick gives

permission, but instructs Staupitz, Luther's superior, that Luther must be returned to Wittenberg immediately following meeting, effectively blocking any effort by Augustinians to hold Luther for trial. Frederick also writes local church and political authorities, asking that they give protection to Luther.

Late March/Early April   Luther publishes *Sermon on Indulgences and Grace* in German, meant to be more open to lay understanding than the more technical 95 Theses.

Before April 4   Luther receives permission from his bishop to publish *Explanations*.

April 26, 1518   Luther attends Heidelberg meeting, presents theses now known as the Heidelberg Disputation, explaining his "theology of the cross." Event draws new supporters to Luther (e.g., Martin Bucer of Strasbourg and Jacob Brenz of Württemberg).

May   Luther gives sermon on limits of power of excommunication; anonymous summary by hearer widely circulated; increases opposition to Luther in some quarters.

Early May   Tetzel publishes theses criticizing Elector Frederick for protecting Luther.

May   *Processus ordinarius* opened in Rome to investigate whether Luther is teaching heresy.

June   Luther publishes *Freedom of the Sermon on Indulgence and Grace* in reply to Tetzel.

Early July   Message sent to Cardinal Cajetan, papal legate to Diet of Holy Roman Empire meeting in Augsburg, to have Luther summoned to Rome.

July   Sylvester Prierias, Master of the Papal Palace, publishes in Rome *Dialogue on the Presumptuous Conclusions on Papal Power of Martin Luther*, focusing on 95 Theses.

August	Luther publishes *Response* to Prierias's *Dialogue*; also *Explanations of 95 Theses* finally published.
August 5	Holy Roman Emperor Maximilian writes pope, denouncing Luther and asking that he be stopped from spreading his teachings before they gain more support.
August 7	Luther receives summons to appear in Rome within sixty days to discuss his theology.
August 8	Luther writes to Elector Frederick, asking that he have investigation transferred to Germany.
Before August 23	Decision in Rome, probably in response to August 5 letter from Emperor Maximilian, to open *processus summarius* against Luther, in which he is to be treated as a known and pertinacious heretic, to be offered choice between recantation and condemnation. Cardinal Cajetan, at Imperial Diet in Augsburg, authorized to act on this decision. Augustinian order also authorized to arrest Luther.
After August 23	Elector Frederick meets with Cajetan, urges him to give Luther hearing. Cajetan does not inform Frederick about Roman summary judgment, but writes Rome, asking for new instructions that would permit him to give Luther a hearing.
September 11	New instructions sent to Cajetan from Rome, authorizing him to examine Luther and make judgment.
Soon after September 18	Frederick instructs Luther to come to Augsburg to meet with Cajetan.
October 12–14	Luther interrogated by Cardinal Cajetan at Augsburg; Cajetan insists that Luther retract views on foundation of indulgences and sort of faith needed effectively to receive absolution in confession. Luther unconvinced and will not retract.

About October 15	Frederick informed about order to Augustinians to have Luther arrested; raises doubt about Catholic intentions.
October 16	Luther prepares and has notarized an appeal from Cajetan to the pope, stating willingness to submit to papal judgment.
About October 16	Cajetan indicates through intermediaries that Luther's position on faith needed to receive absolution can be interpreted as acceptable; on indulgences, matter can be settled if Luther expresses acceptance of papal bull of 1343 *Unigenitus*, that indulgences apply treasury of merits of Christ and the saints.
October 17	Luther writes to Cajetan that he is willing to observe moratorium of statements on indulgences if his opponents do so also, but he cannot make a revocation against conscience.
October 18	Luther composes farewell letter to Cajetan, telling him of intention to appeal to Rome. Luther receives no answer to this or previous letter.
October 21–22	Luther leaves Augsburg during night; appeal to pope posted on Cathedral door.
October 25	Cajetan writes to Frederick, complaining that Luther left Augsburg despite signs of progress in discussions and urging Frederick to send Luther to Rome.
October 31	Luther back in Wittenberg.
November 9	Papal bull on indulgences *Cum postquam* (Dz 1447–1449) promulgated in Rome; drafted by Cajetan.
November 25	Luther publishes *Proceedings at Augsburg*; while appealing to pope, also says his mind will not change.

November 29	Luther has notarized an appeal from pope to a future council in case he is excommunicated; printer leaks copies.
Late December	Papal diplomat Karl von Miltitz arrives in Saxony to negotiate Saxon support for crusade and the case of Luther.

1519

January 4–6	Luther meets with Miltitz; offers concessions, including letter of apology to pope for stirring up controversy (drafted, but never sent), but will not recant.
Mid-January	Luther receives copy of *Cum postquam*; lets friends know that he will not publicly repudiate it, but he cannot accept it.

2

Ethics after the Reformation

Stanley Hauerwas

1. On Being a Protestant Christian Ethicist

I SHOULD LIKE TO say that I care deeply about the future of Protestant Christian ethics. I should like to say that I care deeply about the future of Protestant Christian ethics because I am after all a Protestant. Yet honesty requires me, or at least candor requires me, to confess I am not particularly concerned about the future of Protestant Christian ethics. That I must make such a confession expresses my existential situation, that is, I have never thought of myself as someone deeply committed to being a Protestant.

I was, after all, raised an American Methodist, which means no matter how much you study Wesley it is very hard to take your denominational identity seriously.[20] I have, moreover, described my ecclesial identity as be-

20. This essay is also published in Stanley Hauerwas, *The Work of Theology* (Grand Rapids: Eerdmans, 2015), chapter 2, and is republished here with the permission of the author and publisher. For a more extended set of reflections on Protestantism and, in particular, Methodism, see my chapter, "The End of Protestantism," in my book, *Approaching the End: Eschatological Reflections on Church, Politics, and Life* (Grand Rapids: Eerdmans, 2013) 87–97. My use of "End" in the title is meant to refer not only to questions of the continued existence of Protestant churches but also to the telos of those churches.

ing a high church Mennonite. That description has taken on a life of its own, but at the very least, as I will suggest below, it indicates that I think of myself as being on the Catholic side of the Reformation. I do so partly because, as I will suggest below, I think the way the Anabaptists understood church put them on the Catholic side of the Reformation. That is not to deny that increasingly Luther is being recovered, particularly by Finnish theologians, as a Catholic thinker.[21]

Of course that I have little at stake in the future of Protestant ethics or even being a Protestant is a very Protestant position. Only a Protestant theologian or ethicist would think that it makes little difference whether they are or are not Protestant for the work they do. Yet my lack of passion or commitment to Protestantism as well as the commitment to do ethics in a manner that can be identified as Protestant risks making me a representative of that most despised position, at least despised by me, namely, the theologian as a thinker. Yet given the loss of any clear Protestant ecclesial identity it is not apparent to me if a Protestant can avoid that fate in our time.

What it means to be a "thinker" I can illustrate by telling a story about a faculty meeting at Notre Dame during the time I was a member of the theology faculty. We were discussing yet one more time what it might mean to be an ecumenical department of theology in a Catholic context. My colleagues contributed to the discussion by indicating what difference they thought being Lutheran, Reformed, Anabaptist, Anglican, and even, Jesuit might make for helping us know better what it meant to be Catholic. I was trying as hard as I could to think what special gift Methodism might bring to our endeavors. But then the thought hit me "Hell! I am not a Methodist I went to Yale." I think to be so identified is not peculiar to me but applies to most Christian theologians and ethicists at this time—namely we are people determined more by where we went to graduate school than our ecclesial identity.

My disavowal of the significance of being a Protestant for how I do ethics, however, can be an invitation to self-deception. I am, after all, going

21. For a good introduction to the Finnish Luther, see *Union with Christ: The New Finnish Interpretation of Luther*, ed. Carl Braaten and Robert Jenson (Grand Rapids: Eerdmans, 1998). Mannermaa's chapter, "Why is Luther so Fascinating?" is a particularly helpful article about this turn in Luther interpretation. In short, Mannermaa and his colleagues are suggesting that Luther's understanding of justification by faith through grace is similar to accounts of *theosis* in the East. If that is right it also means then Wesley's understanding of sanctification can be read in a similar way.

to die the death of a Protestant Christian. I know this to be the case because my wife, who is an ordained Methodist appointed to an Episcopal church, and I have bought a niche in the columbarium of the Church of the Holy Family in Chapel Hill, North Carolina. Holy Family is an Episcopal Church even if the name is primarily associated with Roman Catholic churches. I can assure you, however, that Holy Family is a Protestant church because we call the basement the undercroft. That clearly makes us Episcopalian, that is, people who are determined to let no pretension go unused.

That I will die a Protestant does not mean that Catholicism has not had, as well as continues to have, a significant role in my life. Fourteen years at the University of Notre Dame cannot help leaving its mark on you. During those years I was drawn into a world I had not known even existed prior to coming to Notre Dame. I had known from graduate school that something called Catholic theology and ethics exists, but, at least in America, Catholicism is a material faith that cannot be reduced to what Catholics may or may not think. That does not mean that what Catholic theologians and moralists think is not important, but neither is what they think that which makes Catholicism Catholic.

While teaching at Notre Dame I, of course, became acquainted with theologians about who I had never heard. They simply were not part of the Protestant canon. For example, soon after arriving at Notre Dame I found myself on a dissertation committee on Catholic modernism. I had never heard of Catholic modernism. Though I had taken a course with Bernard Haring during my graduate work I was innocent of Catholic moral theology prior to Vatican II. I began to read widely in Catholic moral theology as well as the Social Encyclicals. I soon began to teach courses in Catholic moral theology because I assumed that was something even a Protestant should do given that most of our students were Catholic. That they were Catholic meant, of course, that they knew very little about Catholicism and even less about the Catholic moral tradition.

I do not want to be misunderstood. I did not teach Catholic moral theology only because the students were Catholic. I taught Catholic moral theology because it is such a rich theological tradition. In particular that Catholics had the confessional meant they had to think concretely about moral problems in a manner that was largely unknown to Protestants. Accordingly I simply assumed when I came to Duke Divinity School I should continue to teach Catholic moral theology as well as the Social Encyclicals.[22]

---

22. For my "take" on the social encyclicals, see my chapter (with Jana Bennett), "'A

I did so because I thought those going into the Protestant ministry would benefit from such a course, but I also thought graduate students needed to know the Catholic tradition because it was more than likely that a Catholic institution is where they would end up teaching.

It did not occur to me to identify as a Protestant or Catholic ethicist. I simply thought I was doing Christian ethics. What that meant can be illustrated by an exchange during my initial interview for the position at Notre Dame. I was asked what I would like to teach. Among the courses I mentioned I said I would like to teach a course on Thomas Aquinas. In response I was asked why as a Protestant I wanted to teach Aquinas because Aquinas was a Roman Catholic. I challenged that description pointing out that Aquinas could not have known he was a Roman Catholic because the Reformation had not yet taken place. I then observed I had no reason to think Aquinas was only of use by Roman Catholics. As a Christian ethicist I assumed Aquinas was fair game for anyone committed to doing Christian ethics in a manner that reflected what I thought to be the growing ecumenical commitments by Catholics and Protestants.[23]

Of course the more pressing question was not whether as a Protestant I could or should use Aquinas but rather how anyone like me whose way of thinking had been as deeply shaped by Barth could also be influenced by Aquinas. Barth and Aquinas not only came from different ages and contexts their fundamental presuppositions seemed irreconcilable. The difference is at least suggested by a question I sometimes asked graduate students taking their preliminary exams. I would ask the student to comment on the proposition that Aristotle is to Aquinas as Kant is to Barth. As I will try to suggest below if we are living in a post-Christian world I do not think it is absurd to think that Barth and Aquinas are important allies to help us negotiate that world.

The fact that my identity as a Christian ethicist did not require me to be Protestant or Catholic does not mean, however, that I had a clear idea of

Recall to Christian Life': What is Social about the Catholic Social Teachings," in my book, *Working with Words: On Learning to Speak Christian* (Eugene, OR: Cascade, 2013) 233–54.

23. For my attempt to respond to George Lindbeck's question about my lack of interest in the Protestant ecumenical movement, see my chapter "Which Church? What Unity? Or an Attempt to Say What I May Think about the Future of Christian Unity," in *Approaching the End*, 98–119. Also relevant is *Postliberal Theology and the Church Catholic: Conversations with George Lindbeck, David Burrell, and Stanley Hauerwas*, edited by John Wright (Grand Rapids: Baker Academic, 2012).

what being a Christian ethicist entailed. How could I know what it means to be a Christian ethicist given the fact that Christian ethics is a relatively new discipline and lacks any generally agreed upon "method" or clearly defined subject matter. I have tried to provide an account of the development of Christian ethics in America by focusing on figures such as Walter Rauschenbusch, Reinhold Niebuhr, H. Richard Niebuhr, Paul Ramsey, James Gustafson, and John Howard Yoder. These are substantive figures, but it is not clear that their legacy has been sufficient to sustain a discipline called Protestant Christian ethics. Thus my suggestion that Christian ethics in America has come to a dead end. It has so because the subject of Christian ethics in America was America. Just to the extent America became what Christian ethicists wanted Christian ethics became unintelligible to itself.[24]

Of course the question of the future of Protestant ethics is a question inseparable from the larger question of whether Protestantism itself has a future. The decline of Protestant churches is a stark reality. Of course Protestant ethics as an academic subject may be able to continue in some form even though there are few Protestants and, in particular, Protestant ministers, left to read what Protestant ethicists write. But then it must be asked if one of the reasons for the decline of Protestantism was and is due to the failure of Protestant theologians to do theology in a manner that could help Protestant Christians have a reason for being Protestant.

The very description "protestant" suggests a movement of reform within the church catholic. When Protestantism became an end in itself, when Protestant churches became denominations, Protestantism became unintelligible to itself. No doubt the suggestion that Protestantism has become unintelligible to itself is a generalization that threatens oversimplification given the complex historical development we now call the "Reformation." But then almost any attempt to say what the Reformation was turns out to be hard to sustain. A fact clearly indicated by the question of whether "reformation" is an accurate or useful description of what is alleged to have happened five hundred years ago. For as odd as it may seem it is not at all clear we yet know what happened five hundred years ago even though what did happen resulted in some of us now being known as "Protestants."

24. For my account of these developments, see my chapter "Christian Ethics in America (and *The Journal of Religious Ethics*): A Report on a Book I Will Not Write," in my book *A Better Hope: Resources for a Church Confronting Capitalism, Democracy, and Postmodernity* (Grand Rapids: Brazos, 2000) 55–69.

2. Yet the Reformation Matters

To this point I have been engaged in what Jeff Stout rightly identified as an extended exercise in interminable throat-clearing. I have been delaying as long as possible trying to say something about the legacy of the Reformation. Given the agenda of this conference I assume it is incumbent on those asked to write papers to say something about what or how we understand what influence the Reformation legacy has had for how we do theological ethics. Of course that entails some account of what one takes the Reformation legacy to be. The problem with trying to answer that question is there are too many "reformations," each of which has a different legacy.

It is generally assumed that there are at least four Reformations—the Lutheran, the Reformed, the Anabaptist, and the Church of England—but those descriptions fail to do justice to the complexity that the name suggests. Those reformations were not isolated from one another, which means they often shared more in common than they differed. It is also true that Catholicism can be thought to have gone through a reformation in response to the Reformation. That said I am sure each of those "reformations" have played a role in how I have learned to think about theological ethics though it is not clear to me I would recognize what that role may be or has been.

Moreover, any attempt to get a handle on the Reformation is complicated by recent developments that attempt to put the Reformation in a new light. Eamon Duffy's *The Stripping of the Altars: Traditional Religion in England, 1400–1580* and Brad Gregory's *The Unintended Reformation: How a Religious Revolution Secularized Society* are representatives of this development.[25] Duffy and Gregory deny they are romanticizing the past by arguing that the religious character of church and society prior to the Reformation was not nearly as corrupt as Protestant historiography has implied. They do not deny that the church needed reforming, but they imply that reformation could have been possible without dividing Christendom.[26] It is beyond my competence to assess their arguments though their work

25. Eamon Duffy, *The Stripping of the Altars: Traditional Religion in England, 1400–1580* (New Haven: Yale University Press, 1992), and Brad Gregory, *The Unintended Reformation: How a Religious Revolution Secularized Society* (Cambridge: Harvard University Press, 2012).

26. For a strong critique of Duffy, see David Aers, "Altars of Power: Reflections on Eamon Duffy's *The Stripping of the Altars,*" *Literature and History* 3 (1994) 90–105. Duffy's reply can be found in the preface to the second edition of *Stripping of the Altars*, xxi–xxv.

clearly has implications for how Christian ethics should take account of the Reformation legacy.

There is, however, one glaring, undeniable, and decisive influence of the Reformation on me that is crucial for how I have worked as a Christian ethicist. That influence bears a name—John Howard Yoder. I think it important to call attention to Yoder's influence because he represents aspects of the Reformation that are often forgotten by those who think that the primary concern of the Reformers was doctrine. Doctrine was and is extremely important, but equally significant was the question of whether the habits of Constantinian Christianity should be continued. That question has doctrinal implication by making clear that the very isolation of doctrine from ethics and politics was and is a Constantinian strategy.

I do not want to be misunderstood. The magisterial Reformers' recovery of the christological center of the Christian faith expressed in the language of justification by faith through grace is of singular significance. Yet as Protestantism developed, the emphasis on justification became divorced from Christology and as a result justification by grace through faith became a description of the anthropological conditions necessary to have "faith." In short, the Lutheran emphasis on justification became the breeding grounds for the development of Protestant liberalism and the subsequent moralization of Christian theology. By "moralization of Christian theology" I simply mean once justification was lost as a way to talk about the priority of God's grace, Kant's attempt to "save" Christian convictions by construing them as ethics was inevitable. *Religion Within the Limits of Reason Alone* is the great text in Protestant moral theology.[27]

Kant's account of Christian ethics served to reinforce the general character of how the Christian life was depicted by Protestant theologians. For example Kant insisted that the "sacred narrative," which is appropriately employed on behalf of ecclesiastical faith, "can have and, taken by itself, ought to have absolutely no influence on the adoption of moral maxims."[28] The adoption of such maxims must be based on reason itself. The christological implications are clear, that is, what is crucial is not what strikes the senses and can be known through experience by the appearance of the God-Man (on earth), but "rather the archetype, lying in our reason, that we

---

27. Immanuel Kant, *Religion within the Limits of Reason Alone*, trans. Theodore Greene (New York: Harper, 1934).

28. Ibid., 123.

attribute to him (since, so far as his example can be known, he is found to conform thereto), which is really the object of saving faith."[29]

Kant's philosophical transformation of Protestant theological ethics assumed as well as reinforced the ecclesial politics of the magisterial Reformers.[30] Troeltsch put the matter this way: "The Lutheran ethic is summed up in the following characteristic features: confidence in God founded on His grace, and love of one's neighbor which is exercised in the social duties of one's calling, combined with an obedient surrender to the order of Society created by the Law of Nature."[31] Whether Luther's challenge to the theological and ecclesial presumptions of the day is understood as radical or not there is no question that the Lutheran Reformation was politically and socially conservative. That it was so, moreover, had the effect over time of making it difficult to maintain the truthful status of fundamental theological claims.

The underwriting of the status quo by the magisterial Reformers is why it is so important that those groups generally described by the not very useful name, Anabaptist, not be forgotten or ignored. Of course it is by no means clear who the Anabaptists were. Some seemed to be quite mad. Some rejected the main tenets of the Christian faith while others seemed not to know there were main tenets of the Christian faith. Some would baptize children but others would not. Those who would not baptize children allegedly would not do so because they thought that you could be baptized only if you knew what you were doing. The matter is, however, more complex. For many believers baptism was a norm because the baptized must be ready to be subject to communal discipline.

29. Ibid., 110. Kant is equally clear about the atonement. Thus his claim that "no reasonable man" who knows he merits punishment can believe that all he needs to do is accept forgiveness (ibid., 107).

30. Thus Kant's claim that the "sovereignty of the good principle is attainable only through the establishment and spread of a society in accordance with, and for the sake of, the laws of virtue, a society whose task and duty it is rationally to impress these laws in all their scope upon the entire human race" (ibid., 86). Kant, like most Protestant liberals, simply assumed that Germany was *the* norm for how Christians should live.

31. Ernst Troeltsch, *The Social Teachings of the Christian Churches*, trans. Olive Wyon. (New York: Macmillan, 1931) 2:509–10. This characterization of Luther's politics has recently been challenged by Michael Laffin in his University of Aberdeen dissertation (2014) entitled "Martin Luther and Political Theology: A Constructive Reappraisal of Luther's Political Thought with Special Reference to the Institutions." Laffin argues that if one attends to Luther's sacramental and ecclesial reflections Luther has a much more complex understanding of the role of the church in the world than the interpretation of Luther in terms of the orders of creation.

From my perspective, a perspective shaped by my Methodist commitments, the most interesting way to understand the Anabaptist is to recognize they were rediscovering the congregational practices necessary to sustain the holiness of the church. Harold Snyder observes in his *Anabaptist History and Theology: An Introduction* at the heart of the radical Reformers' vision was the regenerating activity of the Holy Spirit which made possible the life of discipleship for all Christians. According to Snyder, what set the Anabaptist apart from more radical Reformers as well as the magisterial Reformers was an ecclesiology in which believers pledged themselves to be a community of discipline in solidarity with other members of the body of Christ. A solidarity that meant at the very least they could not kill one another.[32]

One of the frustrations that calling attention to the importance of the Anabaptist for how we should be about the work of Christian ethics is there is no decisive figure or document to which one can appeal as defining what makes the Anabaptist Anabaptist. The temptation is to try to make the Schleitheim Confession of 1527, a confession written by Michael Sattler, who not long after drafting the Confession was soon executed in Zurich, the normative statement that defines what it means to be an Anabaptist. That Confession, to be sure, deals with practices that have defined Anabaptist life such as the refusal of infant baptism, the use of the ban, the significance of the unity enacted by the Eucharist, the separation from the world—or better put, a refusal to compromise with what is clearly antithetical with being a disciple of Jesus—the authority of those in positions of leadership, the disavowal of the sword and of oaths.[33] Each of these articles are important as markers of Anabaptist life, but to turn them into a checklist to decide who is and who is not an Anabaptist is not a very Anabaptist thing to do.[34]

---

32. C. Arnold Snyder, *Anabaptist History and Thought: An Introduction* (Kitchener, ON: Pandora, 1995) 95.

33. The Schleitheim Confession was translated by J. C. Wenger and reprinted in *The Mennonite Quarterly Review* 19 (1945) 243–53.

34. Harold Bender wrote a famous pamphlet in 1943 entitled "The Anabaptist Vision" in which he identified as the "essence" of Anabaptist theology and life with three emphases: (1) discipleship, (2) the church as a brotherhood, and, (3) a new ethic of love and nonresistance. His attempt at finding an "essence" to characterize Anabaptist life was criticized by younger Mennonites like Yoder as an attempt to make the Mennonite church in America but another denomination. For my discussion of Bender, see my *In Good Company: The Church as Polis* (Notre Dame: University of Notre Dame Press, 1995) 65–78.

Walter Klaassen observes in his classic book *Anabaptism: Neither Catholic Nor Protestant* what is at the heart of Anabaptist ecclesiology is the conviction that truth will be discovered through a communal process in which theology and ethics are not abstracted from one another. He puts what he takes to be the heart of Anabaptist life this way:

> Life in community is necessary in order not to lose hold on the truth. That the disciple will remain true is not axiomatic since the world is full of deception. The distress of persecution and the strain under which that puts a Christian becomes a convincing reason for not neglecting the close association with others of like commitment. The danger of being deceived and the reality of persecution make it imperative for one to know what is important and basic.[35]

Klaassen suggests that the Anabaptist concern for the relationship between theology and life can be seen by their understanding of the Lord's Supper. For Anabaptists, the Supper was not a meal for individuals, but was a corporate act signifying the oneness and unity of the church. To participate in the Eucharist was a pledge to be at peace with one's neighbor and a commitment to the life of the community. That is why Anabaptists insisted that the Lord's Supper should not take place without the practice of binding and loosing required by Matthew 18. The Supper was a feast of reconciled people.[36]

That Klaassen's calls attention to the Anabaptist understanding of the Lord's Supper, an account that is no doubt in tension with the presumption that most Anabaptists were followers of Zwingli, serves as evidence for his contention that the Anabaptists are neither Protestant or Catholic. Rather they represent a recovery of the radical implications of an eschatological Christology in which the church is understood to be an alternative politics to the world. Klaassen defends his account of the significance of the Anabaptist Reformation by quoting Meno Simons's fundamental conviction that:

> The Prince of peace is Christ Jesus. His kingdom is the kingdom of peace. His word is the word of peace. His body is the body of peace; his children are the seed of peace; and his inheritance and

35. Walter Klaassen, *Anabaptism: Neither Catholic Nor Protestant* (Waterloo, ON: Conrad, 1973) 24.

36. Ibid., 45.

reward are the inheritance and reward of peace. In short with this king and in his kingdom and reign, it is nothing but peace.[37]

Klaassen argues that this understanding of Christ and the church is why Anabaptists are neither Protestant nor Catholic, but in many ways represent the best of both traditions. Though the Anabaptists underwrote the Protestant emphasis on "faith alone" and "Scripture alone" they did so without excluding the importance of works. They also insisted that Scripture was to be read through "the life and doctrine of Christ and the apostles."[38] Klaassen argues, therefore, that the Anabaptists were closer to the Catholics just to the extent they maintained that the church, a very concrete and visible church, must be the interpreter of Scripture.

Though the Anabaptists were obviously critical of the Catholic Church, Klaassen suggests that the very seeds of the revolt the Anabaptists represented were present in Catholicism. That is why Anabaptists, Klaassen argues, can never completely dissociate themselves from Catholicism. He observes, "it is the soil out of which we grew and we have brought with us more from that soil than we remember. We are children of the Catholic church and the sooner we acknowledge it the better for us, for it will help to rid us of our feeling of superiority."[39]

I have called attention to Klaassen's argument because I am obviously in sympathy with the main lines of his position. That position—that is, my general agreement with Klaassen's understanding of the Anabaptist Reformation—was ably summed up some years ago by Gerald Schlabach. He observed that:

> Hauerwas has discovered a dirty little secret—Anabaptists who reject historic Christendom may not actually be rejecting the vision of Christendom as a society in which all of life is integrated under the Lordship of Christ. On this reading, Christendom may in fact be a vision of *shalom*, and our argument with Constantinianisms is not over the vision so much as the sinful effort to grasp at its fullness through violence, before its eschatological time. Hauerwas is quite consistent once you see that he does want to create a Christian society (*polis, societas*)—a community and way of life shaped fully by Christian convictions. He rejects Constantinianism because "the world" cannot be this society and we

37. Ibid., 50.
38. Ibid., 77–79.
39. Ibid., 66.

only distract ourselves from building a truly Christian society by trying to make our nation into that society, rather than be content with living as a community in exile. So Hauerwas wants Catholics to be more Anabaptist, and Anabaptists to be more Catholic, and Protestants to be both, and the only way he can put this together in terms of his own ecclesial location is to be a "Catholic" Methodist in roughly the way that some Episcopalians are Anglo-Catholic.[40]

Schlabach has got it exactly right. That is what I want.[41] That is what I take to be a constructive way to go on "after the Reformation." Klaassen's understanding of the ecclesial process necessary for living truthfully with one another I take to be the heart of my way of doing Christian ethics. I should like to think that way of doing ethics is neither Catholic nor Protestant, but somehow is both. So as an attempt to make sense of this let me end by trying to suggest why I do not think my use of Barth, who is clearly a Reformation theologian all the way down, and Aquinas, who is not a Reformation theologian in any conceivable way, is not as strange as it may seem.

3. On Barth and Thomas Aquinas

As Christians who are living not only "after the Reformation," but, at least if the Anabaptists are right, "After Christendom," we need all the help we can get. In such a situation we should not be surprised that the differences that seemed so defining in the past simply no longer seem that significant. At least in America, denominationalism seems clearly to be coming to an end. Few people are Methodist because they think Methodism represents a holiness movement. Someone may, given the oddity of the difference, be a Freewill Baptist because they are convinced God's grace does not override

40. Schlabach, preface to the second edition of Hauerwas, *After Christendom* (Nashville: Abingdon, 1999) 9–10. Schlabach has developed this perspective in his lovely book *Unlearning Protestantism: Sustaining Christian Community in an Unstable Age* (Grand Rapids: Brazos, 2010).

41. Peter Leithart has located his understanding of what it would mean to be a "Reformational Catholic Church" with which I have deep sympathy. He suggests such a church would mean that "insofar as definitional opposition to Catholicism is constitutive of Protestant identity, to the extent that 'Protestant' entails 'of-another-Church-from-Catholic,' insofar as Protestants, whatever their theology, have acted as if they are members of a different Church from Roman Catholics and Orthodox, Jesus bids Protestantism to come and die." Leithart, "The Future of Protestantism," *First Things* 245 (2014) 26. That is an altar call that I believe must shape the future of Protestantism.

a free will, but that seems an odd place to draw a line in the sand to deter-mine what makes a Christian a Christian.

That we find ourselves in such an ambiguous situation is why I think I find it hard to identify as a Protestant ethicist. Of course everything de-pends on who you think the "we" is in the sentence preceding this sentence. I assume the we is not only the Protestant we, but the we of all Christians in the world in which we find ourselves. The help we need, moreover, is not what is so often identified as "ethics," that is, some decision procedure. Rather, we need the ability to recover our distinctive way of speaking to and about God and the difference God makes for how our lives are lived.

We will need all the help we can get for such a project. Yet if we need all the help we can get then I see no reason why Barth and Aquinas, clearly two of the major theologians in the Christian tradition, cannot be used to help form the future of the church in a world Christians no longer control. I think it quite interesting, therefore, that we recently had published *Thomas Aquinas and Karl Barth: An Unofficial Catholic-Protestant Dialogue*, edited by Bruce L. McCormack and Thomas Joseph White, OP.[42] In his "Introduc-tion" to the book, Thomas White, OP identifies three topics in which Barth and Thomas can be fruitfully compared: (1) How they approach theology considered as a science of divine revelation; (2) Why Christology is the core organizing principle for Barth and Trinitarian monotheism is central for Thomas; and (3) How Thomists and Barthians understand the status of theology in modernity.[43]

White's elaboration of those topics suggest that given the differences that Barth and Thomas represent they nonetheless share in common a commitment to show the difference God makes and how that difference is manifest in the life of the church and the lives of Christians. Barth is clearly a modern thinker but nonetheless he is a tradition-determined theologian who, like Thomas, is rearticulating truths of patristic and medieval thinkers in a post-Reformation, post-Kantian, and Hegelian way. In like manner, White suggests Thomas can be read in a more Barthian fashion if he is rightly seen as a quasi-eclectic thinker who is seeking to widen the scope of theological claims to include all the strands of philosophy in his time. So, interpreted for Thomas like Barth, it is "theology all the way down."[44]

---

42. *Thomas Aquinas and Karl Barth: On Unofficial Catholic-Protestant Dialogue*, ed. Bruce L. McCormack and Thomas Joseph White (Grand Rapids: Eerdmans, 2013).

43. Ibid., 6.

44. Ibid., 14–15.

I call attention to White's suggestion of how Barth and Thomas can be read in a complementary fashion without denying their differences because at the very least his analysis, as well as most every essay in this extraordinary book, suggests that given where we are as Christians, Barth and Thomas are resources for helping us learn the skills necessary to sustain our speech in a world that thinks what we say is unintelligible.[45] For it turns out that if we are to learn to live as Christians, how we say what we are and do and do not do is crucial if our lives are to be witnesses to that which has made us possible. Barth and Thomas, to be sure in quite different ways, can be read as offering us essential exercises in Christian speech.

In his book on Thomas, Denys Turner makes the observation that Thomas, as well as his teacher, Albert, had the virtue of "allowing words to speak for themselves." According to Turner, you can only safely let words speak for themselves if it is the work the words effect that you want to make count for students or readers, rather than the impression you make on either.[46] Turner attributes Thomas's ability to let words speak for themselves to Dominic who took the business of words so seriously he "could conceive of a community of preachers whose holiness would be won or lost in the success or failure of their pursuit of the *bon mot.*"[47] Accordingly, there is an inherent relationship between that community called the church and what is said, that cannot be said if the church did not exist as an alternative to the speech of the world.

To so understand the significance of allowing words to speak for themselves is to refuse to force words to do more than they can. Nonviolence is a grammar of truthful speech. That grammar often is in the form of a silence, particularly when the speech is directed to or about God. According to Turner, Thomas exemplified the conviction that all theology emerges from silence as do the millions of words of theology that Thomas wrote. Those words, the words he wrote, participate in that same silence. The many words Thomas wrote end in silence because "it is through the Son who is the word

---

45. There is not a bad essay in this book but given the subject of this paper I should in particular call attention to John Bowlin's chapter, entitled "Barth and Aquinas on Election, Relationship, and Requirement," *Thomas Aquinas and Karl Barth*, 237–61. Bowlin argues that Barth and Thomas share a social theory of obligation, they agree about its basic features, and they use those features to say how divine action creates human obligation (238). Bowlin also provides a stunning account of election as a form of friendship.

46. Denys Turner, *Thomas Aquinas: A Portrait* (New Haven: Yale University Press, 2013) 5.

47. Ibid., 17.

that we enter into the silence of the Father, the Godhead itself, which is utterly beyond comprehension. For Thomas, silence is not the absence of speech; it is what the fullness of speech demonstrates—namely that, even at its best, speech falls short."[48]

Speech, particularly, falls short theologically. Speech is at once the glory and humbling of theology. It is so because speech must disclose the name of that silence from which the word comes and returns. Turner reminds us the name of that word is God. Turner quotes Aquinas—a quote that could have been written by Barth—that, "in this life we do not know what God is, even by the grace of faith. And so it is that by grace we are made one with God *quasi ei ignoto*, as to something unknown to us."[49] It turns out, therefore, Thomas, like Barth, thinks we are only able to know we are in need of grace through grace. Accordingly, the famous Thomistic phrase "nature is perfected by grace" does not mean that by nature we know what we want, but rather through grace we have revealed to us the depth of our need for grace.[50]

The stress on the importance of speech for Barth and Thomas may seem quite foreign to questions of the future of Protestant ethics. Nor is it clear how this emphasis involves the ecclesial developments I associated with the Anabaptist Reformation and the end of Christendom. However, if our ecclesial future is one that cannot use violence to ensure our safety, nothing is more important than for the church to regain confidence in the words we have been given. For it is through learning the words we have been given that we might be a people capable of prayer.

I think it is no accident that Barth identified prayer as a crucial practice to sustain the moral life.[51] Prayer reminds us that when everything is said and done this is about God. Barth even suggests that prayer goes "back" to the knowledge of God "as the basic act of human reason. Even as God summons man to pray to him, he points to the fact that he has created him for himself and appeals to this determination of his reason."[52] A claim I think Thomas Aquinas could not help but agree with.

---

48. Ibid., 42. For a profound account of church history and theology in terms of silence, see Diarmaid MacCulloch, *Silence: A Christian History* (New York: Viking, 2013).

49. Turner, *Thomas Aquinas*, 44.

50. Ibid., 171.

51. Karl Barth, *Church Dogmatics* 3/4, trans. A. T. Mackay et al. (Edinburgh: T. & T. Clark, 1961) 87–115.

52. Ibid., 87.

We live "after the Reformation." It remains unclear to me, however, if we know where we are or in what time we are living by that description. "After the Reformation" is a description that assumes our history remains the history of Christianity. That assumption reproduces a Constantinian presumption. But if we are in the final stages of Protestantism it is not clear how we should tell the story of where we have been or what we think the future holds.

Accordingly I do not think we know what it might mean to be a Protestant ethicist. In the meantime, however, I see no reason we should not make the most of what we have got: that is, we are finally free. It is not the task of the church to ensure a stable world. Our task is to be faithful to the Lord who has taught us to pray. To learn to pray, to learn the language of prayer, may make it possible for us to speak the truth to one another, for on that does the world's salvation depend.

3

A Catholic Assessment
of the Reformation

Bishop Charles Morerod, OP

Introduction

THE DIVISION OF CHRISTIANS is a tragedy. Part of this tragedy is related to the Reformation, which was of course understandable in many ways, but remains sad on the point of the view of the subsequent division. As the Decree on Ecumenism of Vatican II says, "[Q]uite large communities came to be separated from full communion with the Catholic Church—for which, often enough, men of both sides were to blame."[53] That persons of both sides are to blame is related to the fact that all are sinners: our sins are in part a cause of scandals, but some sins were also involved in the reaction of persons to the situation that led to division. Another cause for that division is an increasing crisis in the late medieval theology: a crisis of scholastic theology as a system, and a crisis between different currents within scholastics—which led at least to some misunderstandings.

53. Council Vatican II, Decree on Ecumenism, *Unitatis Redintegratio* (November 21, 1964), § 3. If not specified otherwise, all translations of texts of the Catholic Magisterium are taken from the Vatican's website: www.vatican.va.

I will try to outline part of the cause of the Reformation, and then assess its contemporary consequences. What I see as the main consequence (and here I am influenced by the story of the conversion of a couple of American Evangelicals to the Catholic Church) is the difficulty to make sense of the fact that "the church of the living God" can be "the pillar and ground of the truth" (1 Tim 3:15). This practical difficulty in using some parts of the Bible is due to the fact that we are somehow accustomed to our division, part of it is due to some premises of the Reformation itself.

Historical Circumstances

I will not spend much time on some well-known factors of ecclesial decadence. Already in the thirteenth century, St. Dominic perceived that the best ways of preaching against the Albigensians was not to send Abbots in rich and pompous company. Of course the Inquisition and the slaughter of Albigensians did not make a good system either.[54]

On the eve of the Reformation, the ecclesiastical apparatus was deeply discredited by the separation between the Church's money and pastoral concerns. Prelates of prominent families were appointed in order to get the money related to a title, but in many cases took the money *sine cura animarum*. For example, during the whole fifteenth century, not even one bishop of Strasburg was ordained a bishop,[55] and only one of them was ordained a priest: they took the money and left the job to others. Not only did this come through as not too evangelical, but it gave the impression that the Church could actually live without bishops—and would even live better. The sale of indulgences arrives in such a context.

When a system is discredited, this opens the way to some kind of revolution, made up of convinced people and of some who take advantage of the situation (with or without personal conviction in the matters at stake). Some princes will, of course, take advantage by taking the Church's money or by using prelates as allies.

Religiously speaking, the crisis could lead to one of Calvin's questions: "Although the melancholy desolation which confronts us on every side may cry that no remnant of the church is left, let us know that Christ's death is

---

54. By saying so, I don't imply that St. Dominic would have been the founder of the Inquisition, but this is another question.

55. See Louis Bouyer, *The Church of God* (Chicago: Franciscan Herald, 1982) 38–39.

fruitful, and that God miraculously keeps his church as in hiding places."[56] In other words: Christ has saved us, but where do we see the effect of his salvation, where do we see the church, in the contemporary desolated situation? Well, it is difficult to know it, but we believe that the church is present, where God can see.

After all, the question is highly understandable when a structure does not seem to fulfill its role anymore. Pope Benedict XVI said some of that in a broader context:

> The right state of human affairs, the moral well-being of the world, can never be guaranteed simply through structures alone, however good they are. Such structures are not only important, but necessary; yet they cannot and must not marginalize human freedom. Even the best structures function only when the community is animated by convictions capable of motivating people to assent freely to the social order. Freedom requires conviction; conviction does not exist on its own, but must always be gained anew by the community. Since man always remains free and since his freedom is always fragile, the kingdom of good will never be definitively established in this world. Anyone who promises the better world that is guaranteed to last forever is making a false promise; he is overlooking human freedom. Freedom must constantly be won over for the cause of good. Free assent to the good never exists simply by itself. If there were structures which could irrevocably guarantee a determined—good—state of the world, man's freedom would be denied, and hence they would not be good structures at all.[57]

Of course Pope Benedict was not speaking specifically about the Church, and in this particular case he would believe that this is divinely founded and assisted "structure." Still, he speaks of how human beings can be related to any structure, and such a relation also applies to the Church: if people think that the Church and its structure don't make sense, they leave it. We see that clearly nowadays, and this is also what happened at the time of Reformation. What happened then is somehow what Vatican II says about atheism:

> [T]aken as a whole, atheism is not a spontaneous development but stems from a variety of causes, including a critical reaction against

---

56. John Calvin, *Institutes of the Christian Religion*, ed. John T. McNeill, trans. Ford Lewis Battles (Philadelphia: Westminster, 1967) IV.I.2 (1014).

57. Benedict XVI, Encyclical *Spe Salvi* (November 30, 2007) § 24.

religious beliefs, and in some places against the Christian religion in particular. Hence believers can have more than a little to do with the birth of atheism. To the extent that they neglect their own training in the faith, or teach erroneous doctrine, or are deficient in their religious, moral, or social life, they must be said to conceal rather than reveal the authentic face of God and religion.[58]

To conclude on this question: the ecclesiastical decadence played a crucial role in the Reformation. Some attempts to reform the Church had been made, such as the Fifth Lateran Council (1512–17),[59] but without significant success. Still, in all human events, crude facts cannot be understood without the leading factors of their interpretation. In the case of the Reformation, the ways of looking at the Church of the time were also influenced by theological and philosophical factors related to late medieval scholastics.

The Crisis of Late Medieval Scholastics

Originally, the scholastic movement tried to reach a certain synthesis of the theology of the church fathers. The typical structure of a scholastic question can be found in Aquinas's *Summa of Theology*, which would start with three arguments in favor of one view, then express another view, and finish with some answer on each one of the three arguments.

By the fourteenth century, scholastics had developed a lot. Let us take the example of the *Collectorium circa quattuor libros Sententiarum*[60] by Gabriel Biel (1408–95), whose influence on Martin Luther is well known[61] One can find there very long questions, with multiple arguments involving all scholastic authors (only a few were already present in Aquinas, and

58. Council Vatican II, Pastoral Constitution on the Church of the World of this Time, *Gaudium et Spes* (December 7, 1965), § 19. The usual translation of the title of this constitution is "Pastoral Constitution on the Church in the Modern World," but I prefer a more literal translation of *in mundo huius temporis*, because the date of the end of the modern period is disputed, but generally seen as anterior to Vatican II.

59. This council has sometimes been undermined. A good assessment can be found in Nelson H. Minnich, *The Fifth Lateran Council (1512–17)* (Aldershot, UK: Variorum, 1993).

60. Gabriel Biel, *Collectorium circa quattuor libros Sententiarum*, Auspiciis H. Rückert, ed. W. Werbeck and U. Hofmann, 5 vols. (Tübingen: J. C. B. Mohr, 1973–77 [+ Indices, 1992]).

61. I developed this question in Charles Morerod, "Le manque de clarté de Gabriel Biel et son impact sur la Réforme," *Nova et Vetera* 75 (2000) 15–32.

usually only through allusions), which means that the structure of a question can become very complex. Instead of about three initial arguments, you may have twenty of them, mixed up with some internal arguments (e.g., argument 5 is developed with 5 internal arguments before you move to argument 6, without knowing whether it is part of the initial list or still a development of argument 5. . .). In other words: the whole structure has become so complex that one needs a lot of time to understand what is about what. The arguments used express mainly struggles among scholastics, with a few biblical texts inserted within scholastic arguments. On top of that Biel often finishes with a *dubium*. Even to eyes benevolent to scholastic theology (such as mine), the whole system seems to have become crazy and hopeless. No surprise that, in comparison, the Bible might be seen as clear, and that theologians might look for some evangelical simplicity not only in the style of ecclesial life, but also in the style of theology.

Luther, who will be able to quote Biel by heart until the end of his life,[62] will reject some contents of his theology (such as a view on merit which has nothing to do with Aquinas's,[63] although Biel himself thought it did. . .). But more than elements of content he will reject the method itself. Since Luther attributes a very significant role to Aristotle in the scholastic system, he also attributes to him a main responsibility in the confusion of the system:

> [F]or more than 300 years now, many universities, and many of the sharpest minds in them, have labored with persistent industry to comprehend Aristotle alone. Yet they not only do not understand Aristotle after all this effort, but even disseminate error and a false understanding of him throughout almost the whole church.[64]

62. Cf. John L. Farthing, *Thomas Aquinas and Gabriel Biel: Interpretations of St. Thomas Aquinas in German Nominalism on the Eve of the Reformation*, Duke Monographs in Medieval and Renaissance Studies 9 (Durham: Duke University Press, 1988) 100.

63. See Biel, *Collectorium*, L. II, dist. 27, quaestio unica, art.3, dubium 2, vol.2, 520: "Actus ergo meritorius quantum ad substantiam eius, intensionem et moralem rectitudinem est a voluntate tamquam a causa prima sive principali et a gratia tamquam a causa secunda sive minus principali; qualis est generaliter habitus respectu potentiae."

64. "iam plus trecentis annis tot universitates, tot in illis acutissima ingenia, tot ingeniorum pertinacissima studia in uno Aristotele laborant, et tamen adhuc non solum Aristotelem non intelligunt, verum etiam errorem et fictam intelligentiam per universam pene ecclesiam spargunt . . ." (*Resolutiones disputationum de indulgentiarum virtute*, concl. LVIII, *WA* 1, 611; translation: *Luther's Works*, vol. 31, 222).

This is very understandable, but unfortunately by getting rid of a method in part degenerated, the Reformers also lost part of its insights, most of all the strong sense of a philosophical influence in theology. With that, it did not become a theology without philosophy (*Sola Scriptura*), but a theology not conscious of its philosophical dimensions. I will give one particular example.

A Theological Question With or Without Philosophy[65]

As an example of a theological question, I will choose one way of looking at human works, and everybody knows that the relation between human works and divine grace is crucial for the Reformers.

What is the role of the works of the priest in the sacraments? The question precedes the Reformation. About the sacrament of penance, Biel was against Aquinas. The nominalist theologian disconnects the pardon bestowed by the Church from the pardon bestowed by God:

> The power of the keys extends to remission and retention of the fault, not in the eyes of God, but in the eyes of the Church. The first part is evident from the preceding conclusion, since the sin is not remitted, but it is presupposed already remitted by God. The second part is evident from what the Master. . . says: "Since, although someone may be absolved in the eyes of God, he is nevertheless not considered absolved in the eyes of the Church except through the judgment of the priest."[66]

In other words, God alone forgives, but the priest declares what God has done. When cardinal Cajetan will comment on Luther's early works on penance in 1518, he will look at the question in a scholastic way: not only theologically, but also philosophically. He will, in other words, recognize the nominalist views behind Luther's views (running the risk of

---

65. The content of this section has been more developed in Charles Morerod, *Ecumenism and Philosophy: Philosophical Questions for a Renewal of Dialogue*, trans. Therese C. Scarpelli (Ann Arbor, MI: Sapientia, 2006).

66. "Tertia conclusio: Potestas clavium extendit se ad remissionem et retentionem culpae non coram Deo, sed in facie ecclesiae. Prima pars patet ex praecedenti conclusione, quia non remittit peccatum, sed remissum a Deo praesupponit. Secunda pars patet per Magistrum distinctione praesenti cap. 6 dicentem: 'Quia etsi aliquis apud Deum sit solutus, non tamen in facie ecclesiae solutus habetur nisi per iudicium sacerdotis'" (Biel, *Corollarium*, L. IV/2, dist. 18, quaestio 1, art. 2, concl. 3, vol. IV/2, 524). The last quote is taken from the Commentary on the Sentences of Peter Lombard (IV, d. 18, c. 6, n. 186).

missing Luther's originality, which on top of that was not fully developed yet). Luther's *Sermo de penitentia* (1518)[67] tends to separate divine action from the action of the priest in a way which is not without relation to his famous struggle against any role of the free will in questions related to our salvation.[68]

Cajetan remembers what Aquinas had said, namely that "it is not inappropriate for the same effect to be produced by a lower agent and God; by both immediately, though in different ways."[69] If God wants to use an instrument, he can certainly do so, without being thereby prevented from accomplishing the entirety of the action himself. Who makes a rose—God, or the rosebush? The rose is at once and without any competition the effect of the rosebush as second cause, and of God as first cause. And thus it happens that God makes a rose through the rosebush, and not without it.[70] A little bit as the whole text is written by a pen and by a man, but at two different levels. The difference between these examples (rosebush or pen) and the way God can work through our actions (as a sign of his love) is that we can act freely.

Cajetan's response to Luther adheres exactly to St. Thomas:

> It is one and the same remission of sin which the priest accomplished ministerially and which God accomplishes by his own authority; in the same way, God accomplishes by his own authority the same conversion of bread into the body of Christ that the words of Christ effect through the lips of the priest.[71]

To state in this way that one and the same action can be accomplished by God and by the priest, each at his own level, implies a whole metaphysics

---

67. WA 1, 317–24.

68. See Martin Luther, *The Bondage of the Will*, LW 33, 35: "[I]t is not irreverent, inquisitive, or superfluous, but essentially salutary and necessary for a Christian, to find out whether the will does anything or nothing in matters pertaining to eternal salvation. Indeed, as you should know, this is the cardinal issue between us, the point on which everything in this controversy turns. For what we are doing is to inquire what free choice can do, what it has done to it, and what is its relation to the grace of God. If we do not know these things, we shall know nothing at all of things Christian, and shall be worse than any heathen."

69. Aquinas, *Summa contra Gentes*, Book III, chapter 70.

70. Cf. Charles Journet, *Entretiens sur la grâce* (Saint-Maurice: Éditions S.-Augustin, 1969) 43–45.

71. Cajetan, in Charles Morerod, *Cajetan et Luther en 1518* (Fribourg: Editions Universitaires, 1994) opuscule XI.6, vol. 1, 347.

of the relation of causes, and therefore of the levels of being (God is, I am, the plant is, but "to be" has in these examples a meaning in part identical, in part different).

This is a debate where theology implies some metaphysics in both views. But if one of the theologians in dialogue thinks he's just reading the Bible, without any philosophical presupposition, part of this delicate debate remains unseen.

This illustrates the danger Pope John Paul II highlighted in his Encyclical *Fides et Ratio*: "Were theologians to refuse the help of philosophy, they would run the risk of doing philosophy unwittingly and locking themselves within thought-structures poorly adapted to the understanding of faith."[72]

Johann Adam Möhler (1796–1838) applied such a view to the reading of Scripture:

> If it is said that Scripture alone is enough for the Christian, one is justified in asking the meaning of this assertion. Scripture alone, apart from our apprehension, is nothing at all; it is a dead letter. Only the product, which comes into light by the direction of our spiritual activities from the Scripture, is something.[73]

This is the application to biblical reading of a more general view: whenever a new idea crosses our mind, the way we understand it depends on the idea we previously had in our mind. It does not mean that we cannot understand the new idea, but that we should try to address consciously the question of the impact of our culture. I would say that almost all contemporary Protestant theologians are conscious of that, but that some of the basis of Protestantism was established without such a consciousness, because the return to Scripture (in many ways a necessary move, even in a Thomistic view)[74] happened by moving away from a system where philosophy might have played an excessive role.

---

72. Jean-Paul II, Encyclical *Fides et Ratio* (September 14, 1998), § 77.

73. Johann Adam Möhler, *Unity in the Church or The Principle of Catholicism: Presented in the Spirit of the Church Fathers of the First Three Centuries* (Washington, DC: Catholic University of America Press, 1996) 117.

74. See Aquinas, *Summa of Theology*, Ia, q.1, a.8, ad 2: "[S]acred doctrine makes use of these authorities as extrinsic and probable arguments; but properly uses the authority of the canonical Scriptures as an incontrovertible proof, and the authority of the doctors of the Church as one that may properly be used, yet merely as probable. For our faith rests upon the revelation made to the apostles and prophets who wrote the canonical books, and not on the revelations (if any such there are) made to other doctors. Hence Augustine says: 'Only those books of Scripture which are called canonical have I learned

The result is, I fear, a certain mindset separating divine cause from created causes, and that undermines the importance of the Church as such.

God Alone, or God with Human Beings in the Church?

I have suggested that, given his own late medieval theological education, Luther tended to choose between divine action and human action (whether God does it all or we claim to be authors of our salvation).

Such a view is also present in Calvin.[75] Of course Calvin insists on the importance of the Church: "[God] has appointed pastors and teachers, . . . he has instituted sacraments, which we feel by experience to be most useful helps in fostering and confirming our faith"[76]; the impact of preaching is related to the church "so long as we continue in the bosom of the Church, we are sure that the truth will remain with us."[77] In his catechism, he says that the Church is "the one effect" resulting from the death of Christ.[78] I have tried to show that in many ways Aquinas's ecclesiology is more similar to that of Calvin than to that of Bellarminus,[79] because it relies on the basic insight that we belong to the body of Christ by grace.

On the other hand, like Luther, Calvin feels necessary to choose between what God does and what we do: "It is . . . robbery from God to arrogate anything to ourselves, either in the will or the act"[80] and "so long as a man has any thing, however small, to say in his own defense, so long he deducts somewhat from the glory of God."[81] When he asks "whether the

---

to hold in such honor as to believe their authors have not erred in any way in writing them. But other authors I so read as not to deem everything in their works to be true, merely on account of their having so thought and written, whatever may have been their holiness and learning.'"

75. I will quote Calvin in this edition: John Calvin, *Institutes of the Christian Religion*, The Library of Christian Classics 20–21 (Philadelphia: Westminster, 1960–67) (4).

76. Calvin, *Institutes*, IV.I.1.

77. Ibid., IV.I.3.

78. See John Calvin, *Catechism of the Church of Geneva*, Q.94, http://www.reformed. org/documents/calvin/geneva_catachism/geneva_catachism.html (accessed June 15, 2015).

79. In a theological symposium at the Centre Orthodoxe du Patriarcat Œcuménique, Chambésy (Geneva), February 27, 2010. The topic of my lecture was "Calvin vu par la tradition catholique romaine, and it is supposed to be published at some point. . .

80. Calvin, *Institutes*, II.III.9.

81. Ibid., III.XIII.1.

Lord works by proper and intrinsic virtue (as it is called), or resigns his office to external symbols?" he replies that "we get rid of that fiction by which the cause of justification and the power of the Holy Spirit are included in elements as vessels and vehicles."[82] This expresses a certain fear that the material world might undermine divine majesty:

> The presence of Christ in the Supper we must hold to be such as neither affixes him to the element of bread, nor encloses him in bread, nor circumscribes him in any way (this would obviously detract from his celestial glory). . . . First, let there be nothing derogatory to the heavenly glory of Christ. This happens whenever he is brought under the corruptible elements of this world, or is affixed to any earthly creatures.[83]

When Protestant Churches responded to BEM (*Baptism, Eucharist Ministry*)[84] in the 1980s, the same mindset appeared. Not only does the Salvation Army's answer say that "We firmly reject the idea that any work or rite can accomplish what God has promised in response to faith"[85] but also regrets that the text "ascribes to the sacraments powers belonging to the Holy Spirit alone."[86] This does not surprise anybody, because the Salvation Army is known for its lack of sacraments (although human actions play a very significant role in its activities). Others express a similar mindset, such as the Standing Council of the Lutheran and Reformed Churches of France, explaining that "the church and its ministries are never in themselves dispensers or sole purveyors of grace,"[87] or the Evangelical Lutheran Church of Iceland insisting that "the preservation of the gospel does not depend on a certain structure."[88]

No wonder then that the famous *Joint Declaration on the Doctrine of Justification* by the Lutheran World Federation and the Catholic Church (1999) mentions some points that still need clarification:

> Our consensus in basic truths of the doctrine of justification must come to influence the life and teachings of our churches. Here it

82. Calvin, *Institutes*, IV.XIV.17.

83. Ibid., IV.XVII.19.

84. See Max Thurian, ed., *Churches Respond to BEM* (Geneva: World Council of Churches, vols. 1–2, 1986; vols. 3–4, 1987; vols. 5–6, 1988).

85. Ibid., vol. 4, 235.

86. Ibid., vol. 4, 254.

87. Ibid., vol. 3, 144.

88. Ibid., vol. 4, 67.

must prove itself. In this respect, there are still questions of vary-ing importance which need further clarification. These include, among other topics, the relationship between the word of God and church doctrine, as well as ecclesiology, ecclesial authority, church unity, ministry, the sacraments, and the relation between justifica-tion and social ethics.[89]

A general view on the relation between divine and human actions tends to undermine the importance of the sacraments, of ministries, of the Church as such, and therefore of ecumenism.

A Catholic view on ecumenism depends on a certain view on the Church:

> [T]he society structured with hierarchical organs and the mystical body of Christ, are not to be considered as two realities, nor are the visible assembly and the spiritual community, nor the earthly church and the Church enriched with heavenly things; rather they form one complex reality which coalesces from a divine and a hu-man element.[90]

This is why John Paul II could keep insisting on the idea that "the ultimate goal of the ecumenical movement is to reestablish full visible unity among all the baptized,"[91] which seemed common at the time of Vatican II, but might be less common nowadays. Many Protestants keep hoping the same, but my question would be whether this is not incompatible with an unconscious undermining of the Church.

In 1963, my Dominican confrere Yes Congar summarized this crucial question:

> [T]he divergence between the Reformation and the Church is still very serious, for it involves the very notion we ought to have of God's covenant relation with men. The Reformers wished this to depend on God alone and to be established directly (vertically) between God and sinful man, as a pure salvation by grace through faith. This suggestion involved the three following consequences . . . and, to my mind, these still constitute the decisive points on which progress is still to be achieved . . . :

89. *Joint Declaration on the Doctrine of Justification*, § 43, http://www.vatican.va/roman_curia/pontifical_councils/chrstuni/documents/rc_pc_chrstuni_doc_31101999_cath-luth-joint-declaration_en.html (accessed June 15, 2015).

90. Vatican II, Dogmatic Constitution on the Church, *Lumen Gentium* (November 21, 1964), § 8.

91. John Paul II, Encyclical *Ut unum sint* (1995), § 77.

(1) Elimination of the reality "Church" as a constitutive element of the covenant relationship. . . .

(2) The omission, neglect, or exclusion of the ministry considered as something different from and more than a merely human organization, or a simple element of good order. . . .

(3) The concentration of all the means of grace, or of the realization of man's covenant relationship with God, solely in the word of God, in practice identified with Scripture. Much could be said about this currently recurring identification. It is sometimes claimed that for Catholics the Church is, in the last analysis, the only sacrament; however disputable or in need of clarification this statement may be, it seems to me that, on the contrary, in the Protestant view, Scripture is the only true means of grace, any others having value only through it.[92]

This leads to another very important question: what is Scripture?

What Is Scripture?

There is no doubt that Scripture is at the heart of the Protestant Reformation. A renewal was certainly necessary at the time of the Reformation, because of the already-mentioned decadence of late scholasticism (although a certain renewal was also stopped within "Catholic" circles[93] by the sad tendency of refuting on each side some good elements of the other side). The Protestant biblical devotion is always impressive: it is still true that the knowledge of the Bible is more developed among the Protestant faithful than among the Catholic faithful (in spite of significant progress since Vatican II). It is also true that Catholic biblical studies received and keep receiving a lot from Protestants exegetes.

The question remains, though, of what the Bible is. Vatican II tried to overcome the conflict between the theologians holding a total absence of errors in the biblical text (in any field whatsoever) and some more historical study. The solution found by the council uses the distinction, previously mentioned about the sacraments, between divine and human causes leading to one effect:

92. Yves Congar, *Tradition and Traditions: An Historical and a Theological Essay* (New York: Macmillan, 1966) 463–64.

93. Of course it is somehow anachronistic to use such denominational terms to speak about the time that immediately follows the Reformation.

> [H]oly mother Church, relying on the belief of the Apostles . . . ,
> holds that the books of both the Old and New Testaments in their
> entirety, with all their parts . . . have God as their author and have
> been handed on as such to the Church herself. In composing the
> sacred books, God chose men and while employed by him they
> made use of their powers and abilities, so that with him acting in
> them and through them, they, as true authors, consigned to writ-
> ing everything and only those things which he wanted.[94]

Cardinal Bea, biblical scholar appointed to be the first President of the
then Pontifical Secretariat for Promoting Christian Unity, said that in this
field "we are all indebted to St. Thomas Aquinas."[95] This distinction makes it
possible to avoid either fundamentalism or liberalism in theology. In biblical authorship, sacramental theology, and ultimately in the whole human
life, one same distinction makes it possible to avoid a choice between divine
and human actions.

Conclusion

At the time of the Reformation, some reform of the Church was undoubtedly necessary, and not enough had been undertaken. This will always be
the case, because the Church is *semper purificanda*,[96] and it will always imply a return to evangelical simplicity, which we can admire in many Protestant communities and which Pope Francis strongly desires.

Among the causes of decadence was the fact that the same Church
had an almost total monopoly on religious life in Western Europe (with

94. Council Vatican II, Dogmatic Constitution on Divine Revelation, *Dei Verbum*
(November 18, 1965), § 11.

95. See Augustine Cardinal Bea, *The Way to Unity after the Council* (London: G.
Chapman, 1967) 92: "The second category of considerations forming a starting-point for
this doctrine of inspiration concerns God's manner of influencing the prophets. Here we
turn to the Old Testament for guidance, and are indebted to St. Thomas Aquinas for his
assertion, after mature reflection, that the authors of the sacred books are God's instruments indeed, but living instruments who, even when being used by God, do not cease
to be their complete selves and therefore act as intelligent and free agents, neither more
nor less than would any other human authors. This concept of 'instrumentality' as an
explanation for the mode of inspiration of the sacred books was expounded by Pius XII
in *Divino afflante Spiritu*, which threw open to Catholic exegesis new avenues of study
and made possible renewed research."

96. Vatican II, Dogmatic Constitution on the Church, *Lumen Gentium* (November
21, 1964), § 8.

the exception of the Jewish communities). Undoubtedly, some internal diversity within Christianity makes this danger less acute. But at the cost of which unity?

These are ways of saying that the Reformation had good consequences. We should not be surprised by that, because God always helps, and does not refrain from using "separated Churches and Communities" as "means of salvation."[97]

As a Catholic, I still have questions about the impact of the Reformation, and offer them as a contribution to dialogue, as much as I hope to receive questions from others. My main question concerns the place of the church in Christian life. Can we understand the Bible when it describes the church as "the pillar and ground of the truth" (1 Tim 3:15)? Does its unity really matter, and if so what do we do? I can raise this question with a famous American Lutheran theologian:

> If this unity is in addition regarded as an ultimate value, an irrevocable gift of God whose loss is unthinkable, then, in a Christian context, the final adjudicator of controversies must be infallible, must be divinely protected against final error, even if not against preliminary falsity. This is necessary because otherwise believers would sometimes not be able in good conscience to remain in the church when it decided against them.[98]

If structures can be too heavy in the Catholic Church, and even in some Protestant churches, their right importance must be recognized, because God takes into consideration our humanity in our salvation. Which unity is possible without the possibility to say together what we believe, and to go on like that? This is a question to Protestants:

> On the Protestant side, synods are the normal way of exercising doctrinal authority. They gather regularly and have a full deliberative voice. Decisions taken by these synods bind only the churches who called them, which makes very difficult a supranational decision. On top of that, decisions can be discussed by a successive synod, which makes difficult any durable decision. One must also mention the considerable question of the representativity of the delegates to the synod.[99]

97. See Council Vatican II, Decree on Ecumenism, *Unitatis Redintegratio* (November 21, 1964), § 3.

98. George Lindbeck, "The Infallibility Debate," in *The Infallibility Debate*, ed. John J. Kirvan (New York: Paulist, 1971) 149.

99. "Du côté protestant, les synodes sont la voie normale de l'exercice de l'autorité

These questions are rooted in philosophical views that cannot understand how God can work within human actions, and these views are anterior to the Reformation. These views, that had been kept together for a while, finally played a divisive role, but stay more or less hidden because of the conviction that the Reformation was simply a return to Scripture. They also impact the understanding of what the Bible is (word of God written by real human authors). I remember that my great Dominican confrere Jean Tillard, a master in contemporary ecumenism, used to say that in the 1960s Protestants' partners in dialogue suspected Catholics of not using the Bible enough, while in the 1990s they asked for the help of Catholics for keeping the Bible. Perhaps a key text in our dialogue could be: "It is clear, therefore, that sacred tradition, Sacred Scripture, and the teaching authority of the Church, in accord with God's most wise design, are so linked and joined together that one cannot stand without the others, and that all together and each in its own way under the action of the one Holy Spirit contribute effectively to the salvation of souls."[100]

---

doctrinale. Ils se réunissent régulièrement et ont une voix pleinement délibérative. Aussi les décisions prises par ces synodes n'engagent-elles que les Eglises qui les ont réunis, ce qui rend extrêmement difficile une décision supranationale. De plus, les engagements pris peuvent être remis en question par un synode suivant, ce qui rend difficile toute décision durable. Il faut mentionner aussi l'enjeu considérable qu'est la représentativité des personnes déléguées au synode." Groupe des Dombes, *Un seul maître (Mt 23, 8): L'autorité doctrinale dans l'Eglise* (Paris: Bayard, 2005) § 392.

100. Council Vatican II, Dogmatic Constitution on Divine Revelation, *Dei Verbum* (November 18, 1965), § 10.

4

Beggars All: A Lutheran View of the 2017 Reformation Anniversary

Sarah Hinlicky Wilson

ONE OF THE NEWEST products from Playmobil, a toy company based in Nuremberg, Germany, is a little figurine of Martin Luther. Playmobil has issued historical figurines before—a series of Dutch painters was a hit, and so was Charlie Chaplin. The Luther toy was developed in conjunction with the German National Tourist Board and the Luther-Decade program of the Protestant Church in Germany (*Evangelische Kirche in Deutschland*), another fun trinket to advertise the gala events leading up to October 31, 2017.

What nobody anticipated, however, was the immense popularity of these little Luthers. Within three days of their release in February 2015, all thirty-four thousand Luthers had sold out. The factory couldn't keep up with the demand, and new Luthers didn't hit the market until late April.[101]

That's remarkable in itself, and proof that not only the pious and the scholarly have their eyes on the 2017 anniversary. But what is even more

---

101. See http://www.newsweek.com/martin-luther-playmobil-toy-sells-out-germany-following-record-breaking-demand-306329, accessed June 1, 2015. This essay will also appear as part of the commemoration of 1517 in *Pro Ecclesia*, volume 26; it is printed here with the permission of the editor, Joseph Mangina.

remarkable is what this commercial Luther toy is holding. It's *not* the 95 Theses—though of course the Theses are why the anniversary date is in 2017. Instead, he's holding a Bible. The left-hand page says, in German, "the end of the books of the Old Testament" (*Bücher des Alten Testaments ende*), and the right-hand one says, "The New Testament translated by Dr. Martin Luther" (*Das Neue Testament übersetzt von Doktor Martin Luther*). Our Luther, smiling blandly like nearly all Playmobil figurines, is no polemical figure, no wrecker of an intact church, no angry young man naming abuses. He's a translator, giving the word of God to Germans in their own language.[102]

I doubt this would have been possible fifty years ago, and maybe even fewer than that. Luther has for centuries been remembered by all heirs of the Reformation events as a strident symbol of division, of the parting of the ways. But now, half a millennium later, even a toy company wants to remember him differently.

Remembering the Reformation differently is the task at hand today, looking toward the first jubilee to take place during the ecumenical era. This was expressed nicely in the 2013 statement of the international Lutheran-Catholic dialogue, *From Conflict to Communion*:

> What happened in the past cannot be changed, but what is remembered of the past and how it is remembered can, with the passage of time, indeed change. Remembrance makes the past present. While the past itself is unalterable, the presence of the past in the present is alterable. In view of 2017, the point is not to tell a different history, but to tell that history differently.[103]

That the anniversary date for the Reformation is 2017 does not make this task any easier. Fifteen hundred and seventeen is the year that Luther posted, or maybe just circulated, his 95 Theses on indulgences, sparking off a firestorm of disproportionate rage among certain church authorities. Indulgences were hardly at the center of the whole Reformation agenda, though; many of Luther's other proposed reforms had been endorsed by

102. I should mention that the brochure that comes with the toy speaks of "the 95 theses which Martin Luther nailed to the door of the castle church in Wittenberg on 31 October 1517 protesting the sale of indulgences—the practice by the Catholic Church of offering absolution from sins in exchange for money." This is incorrect; an indulgence could only offer remission of *punishment* in purgatory for already absolved sins.

103. Lutheran-Roman Catholic Commission on Unity, *From Conflict to Communion: Lutheran-Catholic Common Commemoration of the Reformation in 2017* (Leipzig: Evangelische Verlagsanstalt, 2013) §16.

figures before him and in his own day even by Roman loyalists; and the current doyen of Luther studies in Germany, Oswald Bayer, has argued that Luther's genuine *theological* breakthrough—which was to center the reality of forgiveness on the promise of Christ rather than on either the authority of the priest or contrition of the sinner—took place only about six months later, in a relatively unknown disputation on the remission of sins, which would suggest 1518 as a better anniversary date than 1517.[104] But this is not a matter we get to choose: 2017 has been imposed upon us and so we must respond.

I wish to point out, though, that October 31, 1517, is not uniquely problematic; rather, it is emblematic of a much larger challenge to all the Christian faithful. I grew up with annual celebrations of Reformation Sunday and the lusty singing of "A Mighty Fortress," even though we somehow knew that not all Catholics were bad and in fact quite a lot of Lutherans *were*—still, the day was important and we looked forward to it. In adulthood I've seen a shift of confirmation day away from Pentecost Sunday in June, mainly because it has encouraged a "graduation from church" mentality, to Reformation Sunday in October, which is much better at keeping youth involved and maintains a sensible connection to the Small Catechism the confirmands have studied. It is frankly hard to imagine a Lutheranism that couldn't celebrate its roots once a year in this fashion, but ecumenical rapprochement and some justified embarrassment at past excesses have many Lutherans uneasy about both the annual event and the forthcoming jubilee.

But, as I said, this is hardly a problem unique to us. It is the problem of celebrating any event of history, all the more acute when it is "holy" history. Israel, for example, was commanded to observe the Passover every year, a joyful commemoration of its deliverance from slavery and across the Red Sea; yet this necessarily also entailed the commemoration of the death of all the Egyptian firstborn and the drowning of Pharaoh's army in the sea. Even if the Egyptians "deserved" it, this is a hard thing to rejoice in. Purim celebrates the deliverance of the Jews from imminent genocide but also their turning of the sword upon their would-be persecutors and the hanging of Haman. Ambiguous celebrations, to say the least!

But at least Scripture commands those festivals to remember and make present Israel's history. What of our Christian celebrations of events in the

---

104. Oswald Bayer, *Promissio: Geschichte der reformatorischen Wende in Luthers Theologie* (Göttingen: Vandenhoeck & Ruprecht, 1971) 182–202.

history of the church, after the time recorded by the New Testament? Take the example of the Feast of Orthodoxy, celebrated by the Eastern churches, which plays a functionally parallel role to Reformation Sunday among Lutherans. Often called the "Triumph of Orthodoxy," it takes place every year on the first Sunday of Great Lent because of the restoration on that same Sunday in the year 843 of icons to the Hagia Sophia in Constantinople, putting a final end to the second iconoclastic controversy. Even if we affirm the testimony to the incarnation that icons embody, there is no doubt that political and economic factors played a large role in the controversies of the eighth and ninth centuries, just as they did later in the sixteenth. And ever since 843, the liturgy for the Triumph of Orthodoxy has afforded the opportunity for the collective rejection of heretics—named one by one, to which the assembly replies "Anathema!"—a list that got embellished locally as time went on.

Or again, take the case of "Crownation Day" in the Church of England: once Queen Elizabeth I came to power, every November 17th was celebrated as a holiday remembering her accession to the throne, the Protestantizing of England, and deliverance from the Catholic Bloody Mary. November 17th remained popular even when the Catholic-friendly Stuarts took the throne and inaugurated their own Crownation Days. The Elizabethan holiday's counterpart was John Foxe's *Book of Martyrs*, required reading in every Anglican parish, and the two together prompted English Protesants to thank God for deliverance from persecution and for the gift of wholesome Christian faith—without losing sight of the danger of Catholic oppressors lurking in their fifth column.[105]

Or even take the case of Christ the King Sunday, which most of us observe now as the narrative punctuation to the church year. In fact, the festival is less than a hundred years old. Pope Pius XI established it in 1925 as a deliberate counterpoint to nationalism, secularism, communism, and fascism. Its intention was a political-eschatological one: Christ is the true king, not any human pretender—a point that was probably easier to make once the papacy had lost the last shreds of its own political power. As an added bonus, it was designated for the Sunday before All Saints' Day; in other words, the very same Sunday that Protestants were celebrating the Reformation. Only after Vatican II, in 1969, was the festival moved to the last Sunday before Advent, faciliated in part by the changed ecumenical

---

105. Benjamin J. Kaplan, *Divided by Faith: Religious Conflict and the Practice of Toleration in Early Modern Europe* (Cambridge: Belknap, 2010), 117.

attitude, and many Protestants at that point were more than happy to adopt it.[106] Though not a festival commemorating a church history event in itself, its origins reveal a pointed commentary on the place of the church in human history.

But if there are any festivals that reveal the church's commentary on itself, they are saints' days. These proclaim the ongoing work of God in the life of the church: that His interventions did not end with the Old Testament patriarchs and prophets or the New Testament disciples and apostles, but carry on past Acts 28, into our time. This is a good thing to proclaim—and as fraught with difficulty as Reformation Sunday or the Triumph of Orthodoxy.

For what are we to do with St. Cyril of Alexandria, who grasped the import of the incarnation better than anyone and was the hero of two ecumenical councils (one even after his own death)—yet was infamously aggressive and authoritarian, expelling Jews from the city and inciting a mob to murder Hypatia, the most learned pagan woman of her time? What are we to do with St. Bernard of Clairvaux, a reformer, a Doctor of the Church, an advocate of Bible reading—and an enthusiastic preacher of the Crusades?

You would be hard-pressed to find a single figure of church history who doesn't have an episode, a conviction, or a habit that you wouldn't prefer to delete from the record. The great scholar of the saints, Hippolyte Delehaye, spoke amusingly of "a school of hagiographers who would gladly expunge St. Peter's denial from the gospels, in order not to tarnish the halo of the leader of the apostles,"[107] but it's not hard to understand their motivation. We all wish for a cleaner past—if we have bothered to learn the truth about the past at all—and it benefits neither the pride of our own communities nor our competition with others to own up to our dirty laundry.

Which brings me to a further observation: what divides the churches anymore is not differing doctrine or even differing practice. It's rather our differing theories of history.

A hundred years of multilateral dialogue have proven that we are recognizable to each other as Christians, professing faith in the same Lord Jesus Christ, Son of the Father and Sender of the Spirit, whom we know

---

106. Frank C. Senn, "The Not-So-Ancient Origins of Christ the King Sunday," *Lutheran Forum* 41 (2007) 19–22.

107. Hippolyte Delehaye, *The Legends of the Saints*, trans. Donald Attwater (Portland: Four Courts, 1998) 54.

through the same Holy Scripture. Fifty years of bilateral dialogue have demonstrated quite a bit more consensus than that, on a wide range of topics. Even where disagreements remain, as they certainly do and must, they have become mutually intelligible in a way hitherto unimaginable: they no longer provoke the conviction that the other is the spawn of the devil hellbent on annihilating the apostolic faith. Walter Cardinal Kasper has shown convincingly in his recent study *Harvesting the Fruits* how great the overlap is between Roman Catholic teaching on the one hand and Anglican, Lutheran, Reformed, and Methodist on the other[108]—overlap that could be extended without much difficulty to the Orthodox, Evangelicals, and Trinitarian Pentecostals.

There is only one place where all of this impressive convergence starts to break down. And that's with ecclesiology, which is and always has been both the beating heart and the Achilles' heel of the ecumenical movement. For whenever we say anything about the church's structure, or ministry, or attributes, or mission, we are really covertly asserting our theory of its history, the meaning of its passage through time, justifying our existence as such—and inevitably casting doubt on the other's pedigree or development.

Here are some of the questions raised, at least implicitly, about the direction and meaning of church history. One category concerns the church's origins and how they live on past the first decades or centuries of the church. Are all the initial decisions of the church permanently valid, or are none of them? If some are and some aren't, how do we know which is which? Is it of lasting significance that the gospel arose on the soil of the Roman Empire (and so absorbed its structures) and in the worldview of Greek philosophy (and so absorbed its conceptual vocabulary)? Or was the Greco-Roman immersion only the first of many mission encounters that need to be repeated in kind, not in detail, for example in India amidst Hinduism or in Africa amidst assorted tribal beliefs? Did the first peoples to encounter the gospel in time become the necessary mediators of it, are they more "mature" in the faith, are their cultural adaptations mandatory for those who receive it later in time? Ultimately: was the church already "complete" in its first days or centuries? The way this question is answered (and whether one opts for "first days" or "first centuries") will determine nearly everything else—doctrine, structure, practice, mission.

---

108. Walter Kasper, *Harvesting the Fruits: Basic Aspects of Christian Faith in Ecumenical Dialogue* (London: Bloomsbury Academic, 2009).

Another set of historical questions pertains to later developments in church. The first and obvious one is: *can* there be legitimate developments in the church later in time, or are all essentially betrayal? If there can be, who determines what they are and how? Are some periods of the church more defining than others? If the Spirit led in crucial directions in the life of the church early on, when did that process stop, and why? Is it possible for the church to get seriously off track? Does it get more off track by repetition of the past or by adaptation for an anticipated future? Is treachery possible inside the church or is it only something imposed from without, as the world's history departs from holy history? Why, finally, did the church split—or why did the Spirit allow it to split, or even cause it to split—after the Council of Chalcedon, over the *filioque* controversy, during the Reformation, through independent churches starting up all over the globe?

Though rarely, if ever, articulated dogmatically, all churches are invested in some theory or another of church history, reflecting a philosophy (probably more than a theology) of time and history's movement. So, in brief, you have—among others—an Orthodox view of sacred Hellenism and the necessity of obedience to the canons of the early councils; both Orthodox and Catholics sharing the conviction that the structure of the church's ministry in a threefold office starting in the early centuries remains a mandatory feature of the church today; Catholics adding to this the papacy as the solid rock of ages permitting both the passage of time and faithfulness to origins; a Lutheran conviction that the church itself can become unfaithful, but also that greater doctrinal clarity can come to the fore long after the early days of the church; a Reformed determination to revise ecclesiastical structures altogether; all kinds of Protestant theories of repristination, from the selective approval by magisterial Protestants of various segments of early church history to the Stone-Campbell movement and early Pentecostalism jumping over the whole sorry mess of church history back to Acts in its simple purity; and finally newer, more ecumenically motivated theories of church history, for example trying to undo the confessionalistic insistence on division with the reminder that Luther et al. were aiming at a reform movement *within* the Western church, or efforts to move *forward* to a new unity that will leave the divisive history behind altogether, or converse efforts to move *back* to a theoretically undivided period and church.

Nearly everyone now is also invested in exploring the new historical implications of the explosion of Christianity outside its old Middle Eastern and Euro-American homeland, shifting the balance from North to South and growing at an unbelievable rate. Maybe we hope that in these new missions we will finally have the answer to the question that taunts every effort to resolve our theory-of-history problems: why did the Parousia not come immediately? Second Peter 3 says it is the Lord's patience to give us time to repent, but most of us desire a grander transhistorical narrative than that, and the vibrant churches of the South are some consolation to those of us in the ashes of Christendom still duking it out over the ascendancy of our own historical narratives. Usually we blame those *Left Behind* Series-reading Fundamentalists for wacky theories of dispensationalism, but honesty compels us to admit that we all have our own tacit dispensations at work.

Having by now rendered commemorations nearly impossible, I'd like to argue nevertheless for their vital importance in the life of the church. Certainly there will be those in our midst enslaved to the past—a particular, hallowed, better-than-the-rest, and probably inaccurately remembered past—and there are those enslaved to the future—usually threatening doom but sometimes narcotically promising peace. But most of us, and most of our people, struggle most with the tyranny of the present. Even when in worship we read a holy Scripture that is two thousand or more years old, it is rendered so immediate to us, so much ours, that it is very hard to make it do anything but confirm the present. And all of our denominations and church authorities are very eager to bless our present and affirm our now. But what really do we know of our own time in the church? Like the Heisenberg uncertainty principle in physics, we can't see both where we *are* and where we're *going* at the same time. The only thing we have any hope of seeing with a modicum of clarity is the past.

And that is the value of commemorations: reference to another period can liberate us from the tyranny of the present. It is not without its dangers, and openness to other *times* can make us closed to other *places*. But it remains quite a bit easier to travel through space than to travel through time, so that blind spot can be corrected a little more easily.

Shaking us out of the tyranny of the present is a gift the past can give to us. But there is also a gift that we can give to the past. Commemorations force upon us the realities of history in all its bloody details. There is no excuse anymore for a triumphalistic reading of any given tradition's history or that of the church overall. We know too much not to see the acute need of repentance. And that is what we can do for our ancestors in the faith who, caught in the stream of time and tyrannized by their own present, could not always or often do so themselves. This is indeed our business, our task on their behalf. We deceive ourselves and the truth is not in us if we deny how much our own privileges, gifts, and joys in our traditions and our present are not tightly wound up with the sins of the past.

By way of example let me mention the process that led up to the Lutheran World Federation's apology, in 2010, to the Mennonite community, for Lutheran acts of violence against Anabaptists in the sixteenth century. Somewhere around one hundred Anabaptists had been executed in Lutheran territories during that time, as political traitors for their religious convictions, by Lutheran princes and all too often with the blessing or even encouragement of Lutheran theologians—Luther and Melanchthon included. The idea for the apology came out of the international Lutheran-Mennonite dialogue team's work on writing the first-ever joint history of their dealings in the sixteenth century. The Lutherans were faced with the inescapable fact of their historical wickedness, and despite the dialogue members' lack of material involvement in past evils, simply reporting the history didn't seem to be enough. They put forward the idea of formally repenting and asking for forgiveness. At a Lutheran World Federation council meeting, certain European leaders disdained the idea: those of us alive today are not the oppressors, which renders our apology meaningless. Certain African leaders countered with this argument: we are one body, one church through time and space, their sins are ours just as their gifts and insights have become ours. It is therefore right and good for us to repent on behalf of our ancestors, and right and good for the Mennonites to forgive on behalf of theirs. And that is, ultimately, what happened. Rectifying the past altered the present and opened up a new future for these two Christian communities.[109]

Luther gave us the *simul justus et peccator* to describe the Christian before God. If we want to honor the reformer's memory and celebrate with anything like a clean conscience, we need to confess—in both senses of the word—the *ecclesia simul justa et peccatrix*. No more ideological ecclesiologies, please. No more making claims that have nothing to do with the actual lived history of our church, the whole church. To do so is to engage in ecclesiastical docetism, speaking of a phantom that has never existed and has never baptized or communed or absolved anybody. We have fought

---

109. *Healing Memories: Reconciling in Christ*, Report of the Lutheran-Mennonite International Study Commission (Geneva and Strasbourg: Lutheran World Federation and Mennonite World Conference, 2010).

hard to defend the "scandal of particularity" when it comes to the election of Israel and the divinity of the man Jesus, but we still shy away from it in ecclesiology—unless it is invoked to defend one church as truer and better than another. But rarely do we acknowledge and internalize the actual course of history that our churches have followed, the actual details and particularities of their lives, which no official ecclesiology dares draw near. Let us not hide anymore behind "body of Christ" language. To be sure, we *are* the body of Christ. And among the many other things St. Paul tells us about the body of Christ, he says that it was made to be sin for us (2 Cor 5). Only in this body of sin can we hope also to put on righteousness.

I don't honestly think the ecumenical movement has any future, or that the visibility of the church has any hope, until this happens between all parties—working *in detail* through our pasts together, telling a common story, apologizing, and forgiving. Until we do, the past will remain a tyrant as much as the present, instead of becoming fruitful for us all.

Perhaps by now it seems that commemoration of the sheer fact of the Reformation, and repentance for its attendant evils, are the only legitimate ways to observe 2017. But I'd like to conclude with a ringing endorsement of the act of celebration, too. We must celebrate. The proclamation of the gospel depends on it.

Why is that? Not because the medieval Roman church was altogether a bad egg and the gospel had been utterly lost until Luther came along and found it again. There is just too much evidence of the medieval theologians who formed Luther as a thinker and believer for that fiction anymore, evidence long overlooked on both sides in the hostile confessionalism that resulted from the church's internal violence. Rather, we must celebrate the Reformation because it is our testimony to the good news that God comes precisely to this messy business, this travesty we have made of His history.

This is the gospel: God comes to a barn to be born, God undertakes a healing ministry under a brutal empire, God dies on a cross for the sake of his enemies, God rises and shows Himself on the mountain even to those who persist in disbelieving. To put it more baldly still: the gospel is that God willingly compromises His own reputation, integrity, and purity by being counted among the sinners,[110] by forgiving such terrible breaches of

---

110. This is a theme Luther takes up in his 1531/35 Galatians commentary. Among other remarks to this effect: "For Christ is innocent so far as His own Person is concerned; therefore He should not have been hanged from the tree. But because, according to the Law, every thief should have been hanged, therefore, according to the Law of Moses, Christ Himself should have been hanged; for He bore the person of a sinner

His good and holy law that it raises serious doubts about His own righteousness, as St. Paul suggests in Romans 3:25.

If this is the gospel, then the church can be no different. It is a company of God's enemies who somehow have gotten entangled in His life anyway, a place where He acts despite the tarring of His purity: where corrupt clergy handle His body and blood and where the unworthy receive it; where new life is poured over those too young to have repented of the old one or over grown-ups who request it for all sorts of mixed motives; where the word is preached by those who barely understand it; and where even in the rage and rhetoric and pomp and polemic of an angry friar in a podunk university town, the word of God gets spoken again in a new and fresh and powerful way. History's an utter mess; church history too; of course it is. If it weren't, why would God need to come and save us at all?

God did come to save; and He bestows this same salvation on us again and again in a long historical narrative that is beyond the grasp of any of our theories; and when we see, even as in a glass darkly, the good news breaking through the crust of human sin, *that* is good cause for rejoicing. That is what led Philip Melanchthon in his Apology to outline the very good reasons for an evangelical veneration of the saints:

> Our confession approves giving honor to the saints. This honor is threefold. The first is thanksgiving: we ought to give thanks to God because he has given examples of his mercy, because he has shown that he wants to save humankind, and because he has given teachers and other gifts to the church. Since these are the greatest gifts, they ought to be extolled very highly, and we ought to praise the saints themselves for faithfully using these gifts just as Christ praises faithful managers. The second kind of veneration is the strengthening of our faith. When we see Peter forgiven after his denial, we, too, are encouraged to believe that grace truly superabounds much more over sin. The third honor is imitation: first of their faith, then of their other virtues, which people should imitate according to their callings.[111]

and a thief—and not of one but of all sinners and thieves. . . And all the prophets saw this, that Christ was to become the greatest thief, murderer, adulterer, robber, desecrator, blasphemer, etc., there has ever been anywhere in the world. He is not acting in His own person now. . . In short, He has and bears all the sins of all men in His body—not in the sense that He has committed them but in the sense that He took these sins, committed by us, upon His own body, in order to make satisfaction for them with His own blood." *Luther's Works*, vol. 26, ed. Jaroslav Pelikan (St. Louis: Concordia, 1963) 277.

111. Philip Melanchthon, Apology to the Augsburg Confession, in *The Book of*

So, according to these instructions, let us first thank God for giving us, in His mercy, our teacher Martin Luther. Luther taught us a renewed love and attention to the Scriptures. He taught us that God comes down to us long before we can rise up to Him. Luther taught us the lordly freedom and willing servitude of the Christian believer. He taught us the real presence of Christ in the act of baptism, in the words of absolution, and in the Supper. He taught us a dizzying series of joyful exchanges, between the divine and human in Christ, between Christ and the believer in faith, between the believer and the neighbor in love. He taught us to look away from the divine masks of nature's brute force, of history's winding course, and of the vissicitudes of our own fortunes toward the cross and resurrection instead. He taught us to love the law of God that shows us how to live together, and he taught us to love even more the gospel that makes living together possible. He taught us how to teach others with his catechisms and translations. He taught us to sing.

Secondly, still following Melanchthon's instructions, let our faith be strengthened by Luther's example. For if St. Peter was forgiven after his denial, and Luther was allowed to bear a message that he too on occasion denied and betrayed, then we too have good hope of forgiveness, of second chances, of renewed hope to share the gospel in our time and place.

And thirdly, let us imitate Luther: not, of course, in his vices, but in his faith and virtues: clinging to Christ, rediscovering the Scriptures with joy, remembering our baptism, receiving the Supper, making our witness, fearing and loving and trusting in God above all things.

Celebrating festivals of polyvalent, ambiguous historical events is how God's people have always done it. Nothing of any value in the church has come without cost. It is certainly good for us in these latter days to repent of having inflicted the cost on others rather too gleefully. But if God cannot work in the mess of our history and through problematic persons, He cannot finally have anything to do with us at all. So let us commemorate the Reformation that began almost five hundred years ago; let us repent of our failures on all sides; but let us also celebrate the persistence of the gospel in breaking through all sins and laying hold of sinners, even through that chief of sinners, Martin Luther, whose dying words were: We are beggars. That is true.

Concord: The Confessions of the Evangelical Lutheran Church, eds. Robert Kolb and Timothy J. Wengert (Minneapolis: Fortress, 2000) 238.

5

The Orthodox and
the Early Protestant Reformations

Thomas FitzGerald

I WISH TO THANK the Center for Catholic and Evangelical Theology for this blessed opportunity to be with you today. I am honored to be among you. The activities of the Center are dedicated to the renewal and unity of the church, so that the church may be a more faithful witness to the Lord in today's world. Today, let us not forget our sacred responsibility to seek reconciliation and the unity of the church as we join in this Pro Ecclesia Conference.

Our words of dialogue and reconciliation are very important. However, the restoration of the unity of the church in our time will be accomplished gradually and in a most fundamental way when our statements of reconciliation are both fashioned and received by persons who are first of all open to the presence and activity of the Holy Spirit. And this openness to the "Giver of life" will not simply be expressed in words! It will be expressed in prayerful metanoia, in the healing of memories, in acts of forgiveness, in common study, and in a renewed commitment together to the Lord and his gospel. May this be so!

Setting the Context

The sixteenth and seventeenth centuries are fascinating and very complex periods for the church. Most of you are familiar with the development of the Reformation churches in the early sixteenth century. Perhaps you are less familiar with critical events involving the Orthodox Church between the fifteenth and seventeenth centuries. This is a time when the division between the Church of Rome and the Orthodox becomes more solidified. It is a time when the city of Constantinople, the center of the Roman-Byzantine Empire, falls to the Ottoman invasion in 1453. It is a time when the Russian Empire, dominated by Orthodox Christianity, acquires greater political and religious significance. It is a time when Catholic missionaries are heading eastward. It is a time when a handful of Orthodox theologians sought to respond to theological issues raised by the Protestant Reformers.

The Orthodox were not directly involved in the Protestant Reformations. The Reformation principles never took root in lands dominated by Orthodox Christianity. Yet, the Orthodox were indirectly involved in the Reformation. Many of them could not easily ignore the new theological and ecclesial developments in the Christian West. However, the Orthodox approached these Protestant developments with different theological instincts than Catholic theologians. The Orthodox approached the Protestant developments with a slightly different sense of Christian history.

By the time of the Reformation, it was clear that there were differences between the theological concerns and approaches of Eastern Christianity and Western Christianity, very broadly defined. These approaches became more acute in the Middle Ages. Certainly, both traditions affirmed a Trinitarian and christological vision expressed in the Scriptures and decisions of the early ecumenical councils. Yet, different aspects of Christian faith and ecclesial structures were stressed. Different heresies had developed. Different Fathers and teachers were honored in East and West. For example, the West was dominated by Augustine, Anselm, and later by Thomas. The East was dominated by the perspectives of Athanasius, Basil, Gregory the Theologian, Gregory of Nyssa, Maximos the Confessor, and Gregory Palamas. These teachers set the stage for slightly different understandings of sin, free will, and salvation. While the West placed great emphasis on the authority of the Bishop of Rome, the East affirmed a more polycentric and conciliar view of church organization. Yes, these emphases ultimately led to estrangement and then to division. It led to a schism between the Church of Rome and the Orthodox Church of Constantinople which some date to 1484.[112]

The Council of Florence (1439–45) is frequently viewed as a failed reunion council between Rome and the Orthodox.[113] It occurred towards the end of the conciliar movement in the Catholic Church. It also occurred at a time when the Byzantine Empire was plagued by advancing Ottoman armies in the wake of ill-fated crusades. This fact encouraged many Byzantine religious and political leaders to seek not only renewed communion with Rome but also political support from Western political powers. After very limited discussions between the majority Catholic and minority Orthodox theologians, agreement was reached on such topics as the *Filioque*, sacraments, purgatory, and papal authority. Yes, these are a number of the same topics that were raised later by the Protestant reformers. A union was proclaimed at Florence in 1445. However, it was a union that divided the Orthodox shortly thereafter. It was a false union that ultimately was not received by the Orthodox at a council in Constantinople in 1484.[114]

Eight years after Florence, Constantinople, the capital of the Byzantine-Roman Empire, fell to the Ottomans in 1453 after decades of incursions. This marked the end of a Christian empire that existed for more than one thousand years. It was an empire noted for its Christian faith, its theological centers, its learning, its philanthropic institutions, its missionary activity, and its laws. The fact that the Byzantines identified themselves as Romans says a great deal about their self-understanding.[115]

Did the fall of Constantinople have a bearing on the development of the Protestant Reformations? Yes, it did in two important ways. Firstly, with the advances of Ottoman armies, many Byzantine scholars left their homeland and headed to the West to seek opportunities for teaching and research and security. They brought with them a rich appreciation of the Greek New Testament, the Greek Fathers, and the Greek Classical tradition.

112. For an overview of Orthodox theology in the period, see Jaroslav Pelikan, *The Spirit of Eastern Christendom (600–1700)*, The Christian Tradition 2 (Chicago: University of Chicago Press, 1974); David Heith-Stade, "Eastern Orthodox Ecclesiologies in an Age of Confessionalism," *Theoforum* 41 (2010) 373–85.

113. See Joseph Gill, *The Council of Florence* (Cambridge: Cambridge University Press, 1959).

114. See Henry Chadwick, *East and West: The Making of a Rift in the Church; From Apostolic Times to the Council of Florence* (Oxford: Oxford University Press, 2003).

115. See especially Jonathan Harris, *The Lost World of Byzantium* (New Haven: Yale University Press, 2015).

Throughout the schools of Western Europe, these scholars found positions teaching the Greek language and acquainting Western scholars with both the Greek classics and the Greek patristic tradition. It is said that the writings of Plato were "rediscovered" in Western Europe in the later fifteenth century. We now know that the activities of these scholars contributed greatly to the development of the Renaissance in Western Europe throughout the second part of the fifteenth century.[116]

Secondly, the great educational institutions of the Byzantine world ceased to exist within a generation after the fall of Constantinople to the Ottomans. This meant that students of theology and other disciplines had to travel to Western Europe in search of higher education. Soon after the beginning of the Reformation, the theological schools of Western Europe were divided between Catholic and Protestant faculties. These reflected the distinctive theological positions. The Orthodox theologians in Western Europe had no choice but to study in a theological school dominated by either Catholic or Protestant thought.[117]

This also means that the Reformation and Counter-Reformation discussions took place at a time when genuine Orthodox theological reflection was weakened, and sometimes distorted. Without their own theological schools, easy access to manuscripts, and a community of scholars, the Orthodox were not always in a position to respond fully to the issues raised by the Reformers or by the Catholic Council of Trent (1545–63). Simply stated, the Reformation did not happen at a good time for the Orthodox!

With this historical context in mind, let us now look at three representative examples of contacts between Protestants and Orthodox in the sixteenth and seventeenth centuries.[118] These were not the only statements coming from this period.[119] Yet, they do serve as examples of the state of affairs. The Orthodox were battling Protestant influences in one place and

---

116. Deno Geanakoplos, *Byzantine East & Latin West: Two Worlds of Christendom in Middle Ages and Renaissance* (New York: Harper & Row, 1966).

117. The classic study of the period is Steven Runciman, *The Great Church in Captivity* (Cambridge: Cambridge University Press, 1968).

118. Jaroslav Pelikan and Valerie Hotchkiss have produced a new collection of these texts in *Creeds and Confessions of Faith in the Christian Tradition* (New Haven: Yale University Press, 2003) 245–68. The Greek texts are found in Ioannis Karmiris, *Ta Dogmatikakai Sumbolika Mnëmeia tës Orthodoxou Katholikës Ekklësias* 2 (Athens: 1953) 498–561.

119. One could also mention the Confession of Metrophanes Kritopoulos in 1625 and the Confession of Peter Mogihla in 1643.

Catholic influences in others. These preliminary Orthodox responses, therefore, are not unrelated to a series of polemical essays directed against Catholic teaching dating from the fifteenth century and earlier.[120] Recognizing their inherent limitations, they have historical value especially with regard to issues of ecumenical dialogue Yet, they certainly do not constitute a full exposition of the Orthodox faith either in the sixteenth and seventeenth century or today. In this paper, we can only highlight some aspects of these responses within their context.

Patriarch Jeremias II of Constantinople

The first contact is related to the translation of the *Augsburg Confession* into Greek by Philip Melanchthon. Prior to his death in 1560, Melanchthon sent a copy to Constantinople with the hope that the Orthodox would respond favorably to its content. The first overture received no response. Some years later, a new overture from Tubingen theologians was made in 1573 to Patriarch Jeremias II of Constantinople. Lutheran theologians Jacob Andreas and Martin Crusius actually traveled to Constantinople to meet with the patriarch. This led to three significant written exchanges between Tubingen and Constantinople in 1576, 1579, and 1581.[121] The responses by Jeremias most probably originated with bishops and theologians of the patriarchal synod. Georges Florovsky says, "It was the first systematical exchange of theological views between the Orthodox East and the new Protestant West."[122]

Looking at the responses of Constantinople, however, there is no clear sign of genuine dialogue. Rather, there is a parallel explanation of points of difference. While the responses of the patriarch to the Lutherans do not have a polemical tone, there is a clear indication that Constantinople cannot accept a number of Protestant perspectives as they were presented.

In the first letter in 1576, the patriarch responds to each and every one of the twenty-one articles of the *Confession*. The response is thoughtful and well presented with rich references to Scripture and the Fathers of

120. See Timothy Ware, *Eustratios Argenti: A Study of the Greek Church under Turkish Rule* (Oxford: Clarendon, 1964).

121. George Mastrantonis, *Augsburg and Constantinople* (Brookline: Holy Cross Orthodox Press, 1992).

122. George Florovsky, "An Early Ecumenical Correspondence," in *World Lutheranism of Today* (Rock Island, IL: Augustana Book Concern, 1950) 98.

the Church. As Runciman notes, "Jeremias replied to each in turn, stating wherein he agreed or disagreed with the doctrines contained in them. His comments are valuable, as they add up to a compendium of Orthodox theology at this date"[123]

At the heart of the first response is an admonition to abide by the faith of the church expressed both in Scripture and tradition. Jeremias says in summary:

> Let no one undertake or think anything contrary to the decisions of the Holy Apostles and the Holy Synods. He who uprightly keeps this principle will be a partner with us in our rejoicing, a member of our community and one who holds the same faith. But what communion would one have with us, who rejects the aforementioned canons and opposes the Apostles and shamelessly turns himself against the Holy Apostles? What part could he have with us? Somewhere one of the teachers [of the Church] says to those who strive to be pious: "One who speaks contrary to the things which have been decided—even though he is trustworthy [cf. 1 Cor 4:2; 9:1], lives as a virgin, does wonders, and prophesies—is a wolf in sheep's clothing, who causes the ruin of the sheep." Another teacher says: "It shakes loose something that seemed good to the God-bearing Fathers, that cannot be called administration, but violation and betrayal of the dogma." Still another teacher [Saint Basil] says:
>
>> One who has the judgment of Christ before his eyes, who has seen the great danger that threatens those who dare to subtract from or add to those things which have been handed down by the Spirit, must not be ambitious to innovate, but must content himself with those things which have been proclaimed by the saints [*Against Eunomius* 2, PG 29.573–652].
>
> Therefore, since so many and such important of our theologizing Fathers forbid thinking otherwise, there is only one correction: conform to the Holy Synod and follow the canons of the Apostles and, thus, follow Christ in all things.[124]

This statement, strong and very pointed, might serve as a profound critique of the Reformation perspectives from the fifteenth-century Orthodox. Jeremias laments the fact that the Protestants base their faith only

---

123. Runciman, *Great Church in Captivity*, 248.

124. Mastrantonis, *Augsburg and Constantinople*, 102–3.

on Scripture and neglect tradition. The patriarch affirms that the Holy Spirit has spoken through the ecumenical councils and the writings of the Fathers.[125]

In the second response dated in 1579, the patriarch was less cordial than before. He made it clear that unless the Lutherans fully accept the historic faith of the Church (as understood by the Orthodox), they could not continue in dialogue or hope for ecclesiastical relations.

The response begins with an extensive discussion of the *Filioque* addition to the Nicene-Constantinople Creed of 381. This had been a major point of contention between Orthodox and Catholics since the ninth century. One can only speculate that Patriarch Jeremias noted its usage by the Lutherans and felt that a firm response was necessary. This response essentially includes arguments used against the Catholic usage since the time of St. Photios.

After this extensive discussion, Patriarch Jeremias goes on to discuss free will, justification, and good works. Based on the previous response, Jeremias continues to discuss the sacraments, the invocation of the saints, monasticism, and icons. Central to these topics is his discussion of "Idle Faith and Faithless Work." In reference especially to the relationship of faith and words, the patriarch says,

> Moreover, we should especially know that grace not only of itself works in the saints the knowledge of the mysteries, but also that grace works in worthy ones, who have the power by nature, the capacity of receiving the knowledge. The one, then, needs the other: grace needs works and works need grace. . .Then, clearly, both (faith and works) are those things that lead to salvation.
>
> Therefore, since it is undoubtedly and completely sure that we must believe without doubt, only this remains, that which it is necessary to seek with all one's might and is to be found by every means. What in reality is this? It is this: that we may attain salvation with all that we do. For idle faith and works without faith are both rejected in the sight of God. Let us consider what has been said in the light of the following: for God, who has shown himself to us as being of three hypostases, has also shown this most evident way to us. And, indeed, know also that faith, hope, and love [cf. 1 Cor 13:13], the golden threefold rainbow, when kept by us, effects salvation for us.[126]

125. Ibid., 103.

126. Ibid., 180.

The third and final response of Patriarch Jeremias dated in 1581 is relatively short. He begins his response by reaffirming his understanding of human free will based upon the fact that the human person is created in the image and likeness of God. He indicates that evil is genuinely foreign to human nature, which God created and declared to be "good."[127] He also states that nothing after the fall prevents man from turning aside from evil.[128] Yet, he also clearly affirms for God's help in all things.[129]

He concludes in 1581 by pleading, with some frustration, for an end to the correspondence from the Lutherans. He says,

> Therefore, we request that from henceforth you do not cause us more grief, nor write to us on the same subject if you should wish to treat these luminaries and theologians in a different manner [than the Orthodox Church]. You honor and exalt [the Fathers] in words, but you reject them in deeds. For you try to prove our weapons which are their holy and divine discourses as unsuitable. And it is with these documents that we would have to write and contradict you. Thus, as for you, please release us from these cares. Therefore, going about your own ways, write no longer concerning dogmas; but if you do, write only for friendship's sake. Farewell.[130]

And so it was that dialogue between Lutherans and Orthodox would be essentially silenced for about 386 years. A bilateral dialogue between the Orthodox and the Lutherans in the United States was established in 1967.[131]

Patriarch Cyril Lucaris

Our second example is the Confession of Cyril Lucaris (1572–1638). Cyril was patriarch of Constantinople in the early seventeenth century. He had a stormy career, having served in the office five times between 1620 and 1638. Prior to that, he had studied or worked in Italy, Switzerland, Germany, Poland, and Egypt, where he served briefly as patriarch of Alexandria. During these travels, he came under the influence of Reformed theology primarily

---

127. Ibid., 303.

128. Ibid., 304.

129. Ibid., 305.

130. Ibid., 306.

131. See John Meyendorff and Robert Tobias, eds., *Salvation in Christ: A Lutheran-Orthodox Dialogue* (Minneapolis: Augsburg, 1992).

through his own readings, and through personal contacts with Protestant theologians and diplomats.

Patriarch Cyril Lucaris published his own *Confession of Faith* in Geneva in 1629. It was written in Latin and later translated into Greek in 1633. Coming from a well-known but controversial personality, *Confession* created an immediate negative reaction from many Orthodox.

Confession contains eighteen brief but very pointed paragraphs. The confession accepts the doctrine of *sola scriptura* and makes no substantial reference to tradition, especially the patristic tradition. It rejects the deuterocanonical books of the Old Testament, rejects the real presence of Christ in the Eucharist, and diminishes the importance of the ordained priesthood. He also deplores the veneration of icons and prayers to the saints. Coming from an Orthodox bishop, these were remarkable positions to take.

Here is his statement on predestination:

> We believe that the most merciful God has predestined His elect unto glory before the beginning of the world, without any respect of their works and that there was no other impulsive cause to this election, but only the good will and mercy of God. In like manner before the world was made, He rejected whom He would and the cause of this reprobation is found in the very will of God. . .still God is merciful and just.[132]

With statements such as this, it is not surprising that his Calvinist sympathizers rapidly translated the text from Latin into French, German, and English. Undoubtedly, some felt that this was a victory for Reformed theology in the East since it came from such a high-ranking personality. However, this was not to be the case. It became the most controversial statement coming from an Orthodox bishop in this period. The bishops of the patriarchate deposed Lucaris in 1638. In the same year, he was accused of treason and executed by the Ottoman government.

The confession was not received by the Orthodox. It was formally condemned at local councils in Constantinople in 1638, in Kiev in 1640, in Jassy in 1642, Constantinople in 1672, Jerusalem in 1662, and again in Constantinople in 1681.[133] This process reflected the conciliar spirit of Orthodoxy in a very difficult period and a profound distaste for the confession.

---

132. George A. Hadjiantonious, *Protestant Patriarch: The Life of Cyril Lucaris 1572–1638, Patriarch of Constantinople* (Richmond: John Knox, 1961), 141–42.

133. Timothy Ware, *The Orthodox Church* (Baltimore: Penguin Books, 1969), 107.

Unlike the letters of Patriarch Jeremias and the *Confession* of Patriarch Dositheus, which follows, the *Confession* of Cyril Lucaris did not have a synodical character to it. While he bore the title patriarch, Cyril's response was of a personal nature. It did not come from the Synod of Constantinople. As noted, it was ultimately repudiated.

In producing *Confession*, Patriarch Cyril might have had two purposes in mind. Firstly, he wanted to show his Calvinist associates that Orthodox Christianity was compatible with, or at least open to, Reformed perspectives. Let us remember, the text was first published in Geneva and in Latin! And secondly, he wanted to combat the influence of Catholic missionaries in the Ottoman Empire. The development of Eastern Catholic Churches in Poland had a profound impact upon him. It created a deep mistrust for Catholicism. He chose an alliance with the Calvinists against the Catholics.

Patriarch Dositheus of Jerusalem

The third example we will mention is that of Patriarch Dositheus of Jerusalem (1642–1707). As with other leading Orthodox personalities of the day, Patriarch Dositheus of Jerusalem was intent upon opposing both Catholic and Protestant influence in the Christian East. While having a limited formal education, he had the opportunity to travel throughout the Balkans and the Middle East as a young clergyman. Dositheus wanted to promote a renewed knowledge of the Fathers and to disseminate Byzantine theological texts. He established a printing press in Jassy, Romania about 1676, which produced tracts opposing Western Christian influences. As patriarch of Jerusalem, he waged a constant battle against the Franciscans for control of the holy places in Bethlehem and Jerusalem.[134]

Patriarch Dositheus convened a synod of bishops and other clergy in Jerusalem in 1672. Inspired by Dositheus, this council, sometimes referred to as the Council of Bethlehem, produced an historic *Confession of Faith*. It sought to present the teachings of the Orthodox Church and oppose the deviations of Cyril Lucaris. To some degree it reflects the *Confession* of Peter Mogila written in 1640. Mogila's work had a decidedly Catholic orientation. Patriarch Dositheus's *Confession* is divided into eighteen brief paragraphs (chapters) which provide a systematic exposition of Orthodox teaching against the background of Cyril Lucaris and Peter Mogila. In the

---

134. Runciman, *Great Church in Captivity*, 346–53.

eighteen points, it responds directly to the eighteen paragraphs of Cyril's *Confession*.

Among the points made by Patriarch Dositheus are the following: The *Confession* affirmed the relationship of Scripture and tradition, and the interpretative authority of the Church. It affirmed the seven sacraments. It spoke of transubstantiation of the bread and wine. It affirmed the significance of ordained ministry and especially the office of the bishop. It affirmed the veneration of Mary and the saints. It affirmed the use of icons. It affirmed the prayers for the dead. It denied predestination and justification by faith alone.[135] In this regard, Patriarch Dositheus says of God's activity:

> This grace co-operates with us, and enables us, and makes us to persevere in the love of God, that is to say, in performing those good things that God would have us to do, and which His prevenient grace admonishes us that we should do, justifies us, and makes us predestinated. But those who will not obey, and co-operate with grace, and, therefore, will not observe those things that God would have us perform, and that abuse in the service of Satan the free-will, which they have received of God to perform voluntarily what is good, are consigned to eternal condemnation.
>
> But to say, as the most wicked heretics do and as is contained in the Chapter [of Cyril's *Confession*] to which this answers—that God, in predestinating, or condemning, did not consider in any way the works of those predestinated, or condemned, we know to be profane and impious. For thus Scripture would be opposed to itself, since it promises the believer salvation through works, yet supposes God to be its sole author, by His sole illuminating grace, which He bestows without preceding works, to show to man the truth of divine things, and to teach him how he may co-operate with it, if he will, and do what is good and acceptable, and so obtain salvation. He takes not away the power to will—to will to obey, or not obey him.[136]

135. John Leith, ed., *Creeds of the Churches*, 3rd ed. (Louisville: Westminster John Knox, 1982) 485–576.

136. Ibid., 487–88. An updated English text by Dennis Bratcher has been followed here; see http://www.crivoice.org/creeddositheus.html.

Some Conclusions

We know that the period of the sixteenth and seventeenth centuries was a very difficult theological period for the Protestants, the Orthodox and the Catholics. It was a time when theological differences were compounded by profound political interests. Throughout this time, the various Protestant Reformation traditions were still in the process of evolving. Even within each tradition, there were differences of opinions and controversies.

This meant that the Orthodox found themselves confronted with a variety of subtle Protestant positions, coming from various places with different theological flavors, cultural expressions, and political associations: Geneva, Holland, Germany, and England.

Likewise, the Protestants had very little appreciation of the reality of the Orthodox Church either in the Ottoman Empire, the old Byzantine world, or in Russia. Indeed, it was very different in both places. Here, too, there was diversity of theological emphasis. There were different political and cultural interests at work.

And behind all of this, there was the Catholic Church and its association with the political powers in Germany, Austria, Poland, and France. Relations between Protestants and Rome became much more strained after the Council of Trent. Despite significant moves toward renewal, the council failed to reestablish unity especially with the Lutherans. Likewise, relationships between the Orthodox and Rome became more strained after Jesuit missionary work and the establishment of Eastern Catholic Churches in 1596. Yet, one must find it very interesting that the texts discussed here say next to nothing about the issue of the papacy.

The Reformations did not come at a good time for the Orthodox. As we already said, the Ottoman conquests had weakened the vitality of Orthodox theological reflection from the mid-fifteenth century. But, let us also admit that there was much more going on in the theological world. The Protestant Reformations raised serious questions that had not been formally addressed by the early ecumenical councils, so greatly honored by the Orthodox. Of course, some of these questions had been addressed by fathers of the Church, both East and West. The Fathers did address issues related to the identity of the human person, free will, and the ability of humans to cooperate with the divine plan of salvation. Patriarch Jeremias and Patriarch Dositheus, especially, pay much attention to these observations.

Beyond this, however, new questions were raised about the relationship of Scripture to tradition, the number of the sacraments, the change of the bread and wine in the Eucharist, the veneration of Mary and the other saints, and prayer for the dead. The Orthodox had an historic understanding or instinct about these issues. However, these topics had not been formally addressed by the Church in council. Kallistos Timothy Ware reminds us of this when he says that "one is struck by the limitations of Greek theology in this period: one does not find the Orthodox tradition in its fullness."[137] He further says, "The Reformation controversies raised problems which the Church in the later Byzantine Empire was called to face: in the seventeenth century the Orthodox were forced to think more carefully about the sacraments, and about the nature and authority of the Church."[138]

Here, an additional point may be necessary. The Eastern tradition had been overly reluctant to define issues of the faith. This does not deny the importance of the significant statements coming from the early ecumenical councils. Yet, even these statements, with well-chosen words, always reflect a certain caution. There is always recognition of the margin of mystery when speaking of God and our relationship to him. Our words are limited. And, God's mercy is immeasurable. One is reminded of the observation of St. Hilary of Poitiers in the debates with Arians:

> The errors of heretics and blasphemers force us to deal with unlawful matters, to scale perilous heights, to speak unutterable words, to trespass on forbidden ground. Faith ought in silence to fulfill the commandments, worshipping the Father, reverencing with him the Son, abounding in the Holy Spirit. The error of others compels us to err in daring to embody in human terms truths which ought to be hidden in the silent veneration of the heart.[139]

This approach carried on by the Orthodox led many to make a distinction between dogma and *theologoumena*. *Theologoumenon* is serious insight into a theological theme which has not been formally expressed. The Reformations and Counter-Reformation forced the Orthodox to think more deeply on issues related to *theologoumena*. These were issues discussed by Fathers and teachers in previous times but not formally expressed by a council.

Moreover, the statements about which we have spoken were generally not true encounters between persons holding different opinions. With

137. Ware, *Orthodox Church*, 108.

138. Ibid., 109.

139. Hilary of Poitiers, *On the Trinity*, 2:2.

some minor exceptions in the process, the statements were written and exchanged. They were delivered or simply published. What was lacking were true face-to-face encounters. Certainly, Cyril Lucaris had meetings with Reformed theologians and diplomats. Likewise, there were limited contacts between Catholics and Lutherans related to the Council of Trent. Generally, however, serious differences and the mindset of the day prevented formal encounters in this period. This is one of the important ways that the exchanges during the Reformation and Counter-Reformation were very different from those of the contemporary ecumenical movement.

Finally, let us not forget about the concern for Christian reconciliation and the unity of the Church. The examples of contact between Protestants and Orthodox in the fifteenth, sixteenth, and seventeenth centuries are important for many reasons. Firstly, they remind us that already serious differences in teachings between Protestant and Orthodox had been identified. These differences, it should be noted, were not at first related directly to the understanding of the Trinity. Yet, these differences related to the understanding of grace, free will, and sacraments. Many questions centered upon Christian anthropology. These could not be easily ignored. Secondly, they remind us that legitimate theological discussions can easily be compounded by political, cultural, and linguistic issues. There is always a context. Most importantly, they demonstrate that there were those who sought mutual understanding and dialogue in a very difficult period. There were those who sought to overcome division at a time when the movement toward further division was strong and commonplace. At least, this is evident in the early statements between the Lutherans and Patriarch Jeremias. Yes, the contacts were somewhat impersonal and indirect. So, five hundred years later we can honor those attempts. We can respect the efforts made. Yet, we cannot remain in this complex past. We also need to be faithful to the Lord in the present. With knowledge of the past, he calls us today to contribute to the process of reconciliation and unity today.

6

The Challenge of an Ecumenical Commemoration of 1517

Michael Root

ANNIVERSARIES OF SIGNIFICANT EVENTS can be moments of reconciliation, but also occasions for remembering and reviving half-forgotten animosities. Commemorations of Luther's posting of the 95 Theses on Indulgences[140] have been both. In 1817, King Friedrich Wilhelm III of Prussia used the anniversary as an occasion to merge the Lutheran and Reformed churches.[141] In 1917, the Reformation anniversary was the occasion for the reunification of wings of American Lutheranism that split at the time of the Civil War.[142] The first centenary in 1617, however, was an occasion for sharp polemics between Protestants and Catholics. In 1917, Luther became a rallying point for German Protestants of a nationalist persuasion; Luther represented true German virtues which were being defended in the First World War.[143]

140. Martin Luther, "Ninety-Five Theses or Disputation on the Power and Efficacy of Indulgences," in vol. 31 of *Luther's Works*, ed. Harold J. Grimm (Philadelphia: Fortress, 1957) 17–34.

141. Ruth Rouse and Stephen Charles Neill, eds., *A History of the Ecumenical Movement, 1517–1948*, 3rd ed. (Geneva: World Council of Churches, 1986) 286–88.

142. E. Clifford Nelson, ed., *The Lutherans in North America* (Philadelphia: Fortress, 1975) 373–77.

143. Ruth Kastner, "The Reformer and Reformation Anniversaries," *History Today*

How will the Reformation be commemorated in 2017? The international Catholic-Lutheran dialogue hopes that the commemoration will on this occasion be more consistently ecumenical and has sought to contribute to that end in their text *From Conflict to Communion: Lutheran-Catholic Commemoration of the Reformation in 2017.*[144] The dialogue seeks to present a history of the Reformation in its early years that all sides can recognize as fair and objective. In addition, it describes Luther's theology, again in a way that both Luther's Catholic and Protestant readers can accept as accurate. While such shared descriptive accounts might seem like a small achievement, a look at the polemical presentations of the past indicates otherwise. The work of the dialogue here is a fruit of a more ecumenical approach to Luther and the Reformation adopted during the twentieth century. Luther studies have been, and still are, shaped by confessional commitments. Rare is the discussion of Luther from a theological angle that is not almost immediately recognizable as coming from a Catholic or Protestant author. Nevertheless, great progress has been made.

The choice of the word "commemoration" in the dialogue text's title is not accidental. A commemoration is not identical with a celebration. The text in fact never uses the word "celebration" to describe the sort of ecumenical event it is suggesting.[145] On such occasions, "when Lutheran Christians remember the events that led to the particular formation of their churches, they do not wish to do so without their Catholic fellow Christians" (*FCC*, §221). The "shared joy in the gospel" (§§225–27) that should characterize any commemoration needs to be linked to repentance for past and present failings (§§228–29, 231–37) and prayer for unity (§230). A task force set up by the dialogue has prepared liturgical resources to be used in such events.[146]

Good intentions do not immediately remove all problems and misunderstandings, however, as can be seen in Germany. Not surprisingly, German churches and institutions have led the way in preparations for

33 (1983) 22–26.

144. Lutheran-Roman Catholic Commission on Unity, *From Conflict to Communion: Lutheran-Catholic Common Commemoration of the Reformation in 2017* (Leipzig: Evangelische Verlagsanstalt, 2013); hereafter cited as *FCC*.

145. The word "celebrate" does appear twice (*FCC*, §§224–25), but in both cases to indicate what aspects of the Reformation Lutherans wish to celebrate.

146. Liturgical Task Force of the Lutheran-Roman Catholic Commission on Unity, *Common Prayer: From Conflict to Communion; Common Commemoration of the the Reformation in 2017* (Geneva: Lutheran World Federation, 2016).

2017. State, church, and cultural institutions have been participating in the "Luther decade" since 2008.[147] The Evangelical Church in Germany (EKD), which includes the various regional Lutheran, United, and Reformed churches in Germany, has plans for a large "Reformation Jubilee" (*Reformationsjubiläum*) in October 2017. The word "jubilee" creates problems for Catholics, however.[148] In 2012, Cardinal Kurt Koch, president of the Pontifical Council for Promoting Christian Unity, doubted in an interview whether Catholics could participate in such a "jubilee." We should "not speak of a 'jubilee,'" he said, "but of a Reformation commemoration, for we cannot celebrate a sin."[149] This remark, understandably, was not well received in Protestant circles.

In 2014, the Council of the EKD released a theological "foundation text" (*Grundlagentext*) for the 2017 events, entitled *Rechtfertigung und Freiheit* (*Justification and Freedom*).[150] The text sought to expound "the central theme of the Reformation, then and now": justification. In particular, it sought to portray the Reformation's understanding of justification as a crucial contributor to, and corrective element within, the modern development of freedom. While the text opens with an introduction from the chair of the EKD Council expressing a desire to celebrate the Reformation in ecumenical breadth,[151] the text goes on for more than one hundred pages to discuss justification without a single explicit mention or citation of the *Joint Declaration on the Doctrine of Justification*, the agreement on justification between the Catholic Church and the Lutheran World Federation.

---

147. See http://www.luther2017.de/en/. Unhelpfully, the commission for the decade had almost no non-Protestant participation. See Hartmut Lehmann, "Unterschiedliche Erwartungen an das Reformationsjubiläum 2017," in *Ratlos vor dem Reformationsjubiläum?* (Leipzig: Evangelische Verlagsanstalt, 2011) 22–23.

148. See, e.g., Gerhard Ludwig Müller, "In gemeinsamer Verantwortung: Anfragen an das Reformationsjubiläum 2017," in *Ratlos vor dem Reformationsjubiläum?* (Leipzig: Evangelische Verlagsanstalt, 2011) 121–22.

149. "nicht von einem 'Jubiläum' sprechen, sondern von einem Reformations-Gedenken, denn wir können nicht eine Sünde feiern." Katholischer Nachrichtendienst, April 24, 2012, http://www.kath.net/news/36255.

150. *Rechtfertigung und Freiheit: 500 Jahre Reformation 2017. Ein Grundlagentext des Rates der Evangelischen Kirche in Deutschland (EKD)* (Gütersloh: Gütersloher Verlagshaus, 2014) Hereafter cited as *RF*.

151. The word "celebrate" (*feiern*) is italicized in the original text. In light of the just noted remark of Cardinal Koch, this emphasis cannot be seen as accidental and issues a challenge.

This absence produced sharp reactions from German Catholic leaders.[152] In addition the text's presentation of the Reformation understanding of justification stressed the "exclusive particles"—Christ alone, grace alone, word alone, Scripture alone, faith alone—in ways that implicitly contrasted the Reformation understanding with Catholic teaching.[153] Wolfgang Thönissen, director of the Johann-Adam-Möhler Institute, the ecumenical institute of the German Catholic Bishops' Conference, wondered if it made sense for Catholics to accept invitations to Reformation anniversary events after the publication of this text.[154]

The storms created by these events blew over, and in May 2015 the EKD and the German Catholic Bishops' Conference announced a series of common commemorative events in 2016 and 2017.[155] What the dustups show is how easily old patterns of speech reassert themselves, calling forth misunderstanding. Stereotypes die hard.

In this essay, I want to point to some of the challenges that an ecumenical commemoration of 2017 must face and some of the pitfalls that such commemorations should avoid.

A. Historical Challenges

Any 2017 commemoration will to some degree have an historical reference. Some may place little focus on the events of 1517 and center on the state and future of contemporary Protestantism.[156] Nevertheless, the occasion

152. Cardinal Walter Kasper, former President of the Pontifical Council for Promoting Christian Unity, declared himself "disappointed" and "shocked." See http://de.radiovaticana.va/storico/2014/06/24/kardinal_kasper_%E2%80%9Eentt%C3%A4u scht%E2%80%9C_und_%E2%80%9Eentsetzt%E2%80%9C_%C3%BCber_ekd-papier/ted-808944. The *Joint Declaration* was implicitly mentioned on p. 39 of the text. Catholic respondents were probably aware that the chair of the committee that produced *RF*, Christoph Markschies of the Humboldt University in Berlin, had signed a protest letter rejecting the *Joint Declaration*. See Friedrich Hauschildt and Udo Hahn, *Die Gemeinsame Erklärung zur Rechtfertigungslehre: Dokumentation des Entstehungs- und Rezeptionsprozesses* (Göttingen: Vandenhoeck & Ruprecht, 2009) 944–49.

153. Christ alone, not Mary and the saints (*RF*, p. 55); grace alone, not "the medieval understanding of grace as only one stage in the process of justification" (*RF*, p. 63, an odd understanding of *the* medieval understandings of grace, at best), etc.

154. Sandra Stalinski, "EKD-Papier spaltet die Kirchen," http://www.deutschlandfunk.de/reformationsjubilaeum-2017-ekd-papier-spaltet-die-kirchen.886.de.html?dram:article_id=291296.

155. http://www.ekd.de/presse/pm114_2015_gemeinsames_christusfest2017.html.

156. The Lutheran World Federation has planned such an approach. See https://2017.lutheranworld.org/.

for the commemoration lies in Luther's action in 1517. Just what that action was is an undecided (and probably undecidable) historical question. Did Luther nail the 95 Theses on indulgences to the door of the Castle Church? The earliest account that he did so comes from the early 1540s, twenty-five years after the event. We have no statement from Luther or from any eyewitness that he did so. Evidence can be cited that would lead one to think he did or that he didn't. Scholars still disagree on the question, although we know for certain that he wrote a letter to Archbishop Albrecht of Magdeburg, protesting the indulgence campaign, on October 31st and that Luther himself later cited October 31st as the day on which his protest had begun.[157]

The question "what actually happened?" while interesting in itself, is not what I would call a challenge to a contemporary ecumenical commemoration. More important are the ways the commemoration might distort the balanced historical reading of the Reformation that is needed.

First, a focus on Luther and the events of 1517 can make us forget that the Reformation was a great deal larger than Luther. The precise relation of Zwingli's initiative in Switzerland to Luther's in Saxony is a complex historical question, but the Reformed movement which takes its start with Zwingli became, even within Luther's lifetime, a distinct and on some points conflicting theological and ecclesiastical program of reform. Protestantism in the United States is far more Reformed than Lutheran in its background and instincts. The Reformation may have begun with Luther, but it became a highly variegated movement.

Second, even if the focus is Lutheran, Luther must not be confused with the Lutheran Reformation, a much larger phenomenon with both theological and non-theological roots. The course of the Lutheran Reformation was not simply determined by Luther; the role of the princes and city councils, with specific political and economic interests, should not be obscured.

Finally, even if the focus is on Luther, might an emphasis on October 31, 1517 distort the historical picture? Luther's step into the public arena on that date is of great significance. The public debate set off by the 95 Theses propelled Luther forward into what became the Reformation. As a point of departure, the importance of the date is hard to exaggerate. The temptation,

---

157. See Volker Leppin, "31. Oktober 1517—Der symbolische Anfang der Reformation und die lutherische Festkultur," in *Tage der Revolution—Feste der Nation*, ed. Rolf Gröschner and Wolfgang Reinhard (Tübingen: Mohr Siebeck, 2010) 55–59.

however, is to see the event as a sort of seed whose DNA shapes and explains what comes afterward. The originating event must also be determinative of what happens afterwards. This tendency to read back into 1517 a meaning that was not there was exacerbated by the pursuit in the twentieth century of a "Reformation breakthrough" in Luther's thought sometime around 1517, a breakthrough to an evangelical understanding that would then remain the constant, determining center of his later theology.

We now have a much more nuanced picture of Luther's theological development in the formative years between his first writings and the appearance of a relatively firm Reformation theology around 1521.[158] To label his theology at the time of the 95 Theses as simply pre-Reformation would be inaccurate. Nevertheless, the Theses do not embody the doctrine of justification through identification[159] with the righteousness of Christ that would remain central for Luther's theology from an early text such as the sermon on "Two Kinds of Righteousness"[160] through the rest of his career.[161]

A temptation for those interested in a deeper, but still popular, commemoration of 1517 will be an engagement with the content of the Theses and with the theology of indulgences. The Theses themselves are certainly worth close examination, though their content does not go far beyond what others had said at the time. The difficulty lies in keeping the right balance, both historically and theologically. Historically, while indulgences were the catalyst for Luther's protest, the debate quickly shifted to more comprehensive questions about authority in the church and about the nature of salvation. When Luther met Cardinal Cajetan at Augsburg in October

---

158. See especially Berndt Hamm, *The Early Luther: Stages in a Reformation Reorientation*, trans. Martin J. Lohrmann (Grand Rapids: Eerdmans, 2014).

159. I use the term "identification" here to point to the complex interweaving of the language of imputation and of participation in Luther's understanding of the relation of the still-sinful justified to the righteousness of Christ.

160. Martin Luther, "Two Kinds of Righteousness," in vol. 31 of *Luther's Works*, ed. Harold J. Grimm, trans. Lowell J. Satre (Philadelphia: Fortress, 1957) 293–306. The dating of this text is uncertain, but 1518 seems the most likely date of authorship.

161. For the theology of the Theses, see especially Berndt Hamm, "The Ninety-Five Theses: A Reformation Text in the Context of Luther's Early Theology of Repentance," in *The Early Luther: Stages in a Reformation Reorientation*, trans. Martin J. Lohrmann (Grand Rapids: Eerdmans, 2014) 85–109. Helpful for understanding Luther's understanding of indulgences at this time also is Jared Wicks, "Luther's Treatise on Indulgences, 1517," in *Luther's Reform: Studies on Conversion and the Church* (Mainz: P. von Zabern, 1992) 87–116.

1518, he already thought that indulgences were tangential to the real issues at stake.[162] Indulgences had significance as one form of a larger problem, an exteriorization of the mediation of grace that seemed to reinforce a *quid pro quo* and *do ut des* understanding of the Christian life, but as a distinct issue, they were of passing significance.

The theology of indulgences has a simple basis. Penitent Christians are not alone in their struggle with the effects of past sins and their pursuit of present renewal. The prayers of Christ, Mary, and the saints are with them, and, because of the merits of Christ, Mary, and the saints, the prayers of the righteous "availeth much" (Jas 5:16 KJV). The details of the theology of indulgences, however, are complex: the relation of indulgences to the power of the keys, what is meant by "the treasury of merits," the relation of indulgences to purgatory.[163] The possibilities for misunderstanding are many. Without careful work, a focus on indulgences on discussions related to the 1517 anniversary may not further Christian understanding.

B. Ecumenical Challenges

Commemorations of the beginning of the Reformation face challenges beyond those related to the presentation of history. Other challenges are more directly ecumenical.

1. Stereotypes and Standard Narratives

An obvious challenge any commemoration with an ecumenical intent faces is how to tell the story of the events of the Reformation without reinforcing divisive caricatures and stereotypes. This challenge, central to the project embodied in *From Conflict to Communion*, may be more difficult than

162. Martin Luther, "The Proceedings at Augsburg," in vol. 31 of *Luther's Works*, ed. Harold J. Grimm (Philadelphia: Fortress, 1957) 278.

163. The most important and comprehensive recent magisterial text on indulgences is Paul VI, "Apostolic Constitution on the Revision of Indulgences [*Indulgentiarum Doctrina*]," in vol. 1 of *Vatican Council II: The Conciliar and Post-conciliar Documents*, ed. Austin Flannery, Vatican Collection (Northport, NY: Costello, 1975) 62–79. A useful popular presentation is John Paul II, "Indulgences Are an Expression of God's Mercy," *L'Osservatore Romano (Weekly English Edition)*, October 6, 1999, 15. My own summary of the theology of indulgences and the ecumenical issues they raise can be found in Michael Root, "Indulgences as Ecumenical Barometer: Penitence and Unity in the Christian Life," *Bulletin of the Centro Pro Unione (Rome)* 39 (2011) 3–9.

imagined. Anniversary commemorations of historical events are rarely simply about the event being commemorated. They are also about the present identity of the group doing the commemorating. Fourth of July festivities are as much about what it means to be an American today as they are about what happened on July 4, 1776. Historically, the same has been true of past commemorations of 1517.[164]

As recent events have already shown, the intertwining of a commemoration of 1517 with concerns for what it means to be Protestant today have an inherent tendency to call forth what Catholics will tend to see as a return to unhelpful and false stereotypes. The problem is that the Reformation, especially the early Reformation, was a protest and protests are inherently oppositional. A protest is a protest *against* something. What is being opposed and how that opposition is understood shapes the character of the protest. Conversely, ingredient in the protest is a picture of what is being opposed. The opposition to this implied other is ingredient in the logic of the protest.

This picture of the implied Other implied in a protest may or may not be accurate. A protest may be based on a misunderstanding or a partial understanding. It may or may not correspond to the self-understanding of the other. Even if this picture is accurate at the initial time of a protest, the Other may change over time and the implied picture come to be false.

Can a Reformation commemoration which is linked to the early years of the Reformation avoid falling back into the oppositional logic of the original protest? If the commemoration also serves as an opportunity for affirming or subtly redefining Protestant identity, can that affirmation or redefinition avoid constructing such identity in a contrastive way, a way in which essential to being Protestant is a contrast to being Catholic?[165] The contrast becomes even more problematic if the contrast is seen as implying a construction of Catholicism which Catholics will see as inaccurate or prejudicial.

I noted above the way this problem arose with the German Protestant text *Rechtfertigung und Freiheit*. Despite an apparent concern to avoid ecumenical problems, the text's presentation of a Protestant identity as a

164. The relation of past commemorations to concerns for present identity is explored in Leppin, "31. Oktober 1517—Der symbolische Anfang der Reformation und die lutherische Festkultur," 60–68.

165. Michael Root, "Beyond Contrast: The Past, Present, and Future of Lutheran Theology," *Trinity Seminary Review* 22 (2001) 81–90.

"church of freedom" implied a contrast with a Catholic thought and practice which inevitably must constitute a "church of unfreedom."

The Lutheran World Federation's (LWF) preparations have a similar problem. The LWF commemoration is focused more on the present state of international Lutheranism than on the events of 1517. The tagline for the commemoration is "Liberated by God's Grace." Unfortunately, the subthemes are linked by the phrase "Not for Sale": Salvation—Not for Sale; Creation—Not for Sale; Human Beings—Not for Sale. The positive message is admirable; in the context of a commemoration of 1517, however, the choice of words is regrettable. A contrast is called to mind with the aggressive marketing of indulgences, understood as the sale of salvation. The Catholic scholar may judge that, whatever real abuses had entered the practice of indulgences in the late fifteenth and early sixteenth centuries, they did not represent the sale of salvation and that ecumenical understanding is not furthered.

2. New Problems

A different ecumenical challenge arises in relation to the commemoration and the present obstacles to fuller communion. The temptation for ecumenical discussions related to the commemoration is to focus on the issues of the sixteenth century that were important for the Reformation division. Of course, present relations among the churches and the issues of the sixteenth century are not unrelated. Ecumenical dialogues between Catholics on the one hand and Lutherans, Reformed, and Anglicans on the other have tended to focus on the classical doctrinal issues that arose in the Reformation and rightly so. The doctrinal issues of the Reformation were and are important. But the Catholic Church and its theology today are not exactly the same as they were at the Council of Trent and the Lutheran and Reformed churches and theology are not what they were in Wittenberg, Geneva, and Zürich in the mid-sixteenth century. New questions have arisen, e.g., about sexuality, and even traditional positions may be understood in a new way. The conversation over justification that a Catholic and a Lutheran theologian would have today would be different from one that might have occurred on the same topic between Bellarmine and Gerhard in the early seventeenth century or between Melanchthon and Contarini in the early 1540s. A certain air of unreality clings to the dialogues if they fail to recognize those differences.

3. An Overemphasis on the Conceptual

A more subtle temptation presented by the commemoration is a focus on theology and differences over theology as the crucial obstacles to greater present unity. For Luther, the Reformation was about theology, even more so than it was for Calvin, who had a more comprehensive plan for Church reform. But Luther's theological commitments do not fully explain what was church-dividing within the Reformation or what is perhaps of decisive importance in the relations among the churches today. A mistake to which theology professors are particularly susceptible is thinking that ecumenism is about the relation between concepts or theological systems or, even worse, relations between professors. Ecumenism is finally about relations between churches, concrete communities of human beings, who are organized and act in accord with deeply held beliefs, but whose communal existence is not reducible to those beliefs. The ecumenical question is not finally about the relation of Luther's theology to some construct we might call Catholic theology, but about the relation of the Protestant churches that came out of the Reformation to the Catholic Church. Will a commemoration of 1517 help in that ecumenical task? Will it shift attention away from present neuralgic problems?

Let me give an example of the sort of ecumenical problem that is rooted to a degree in the social history of the Reformation, but distant from Luther and theology. In the United States today, perhaps in the North Atlantic world generally, we face a growing distance between the implicit morality of the dominant culture and what has up to this time been traditional Christian ethics. Friction is in various ways increasing between some churches and the larger society. For example, the Catholic University of America, where this conference is being held, is engaged in a series of legal arguments with government agencies over government mandates which the university judges it cannot as a Catholic institution accept in good conscience. In this new context of tension, a particular weight falls on how different churches relate to the larger culture. Do the churches have the social and cultural resources to resist an unacceptable accommodation to aspects of modern society that are finally incompatible with a commitment to a Christian way of life?

If this question is important, then a Catholic may have other questions about the sixteenth-century Reformation than straightforwardly theological ones, questions about the way the Reformation fits into the late-medieval and early modern history of the relation between church and society. Was something lost in the churches' ability to live counterculturally when the religious orders were eliminated, along with a celibate clergy, and churches came more directly under the control of state authorities? Did the minority, non-established status of many Reformed churches in Europe give the Reformed tradition a greater capacity to resist social trends than is present in the Lutheran and Anglican traditions, both of which were almost always established churches? These questions have a theological aspect; they are ecclesiological questions. Their ecumenical significance, however, may only become clear when their social significance for the present situation is taken into account. I ask those questions gently, but frankly, as someone who is an outsider to the mainstream Reformation traditions, but I think it is an important question.

C. Normal Ecumenism

The greatest challenge for an ecumenical commemoration of the beginning of the Reformation is a far more intractable reality: the seeming impasse that has brought ecumenical progress between Protestant and Catholic churches to a standstill. The first post-Vatican II decades brought major, even revolutionary advances. Radically new forms of Anglican-Catholic and Lutheran-Catholic unity seemed possible.[166] Dialogues recorded surprising levels of agreement on many issues, especially those on salvation and its mediation, culminating in the Catholic-Lutheran *Joint Declaration on the Doctrine of Justification* of 1999.[167] On issues of church and ministry, however, progress has proven elusive. Without progress on these issues, little change occurs in the life of the actually existing churches.

The ecumenical situation of the last few decades has thus produced frustration. What happened to the new possibilities that seemed so imminent? Are we now in an ecumenical winter, frozen until some new spring thaws out the pack ice impeding progress?

These attitudes create their own challenges for an ecumenical commemoration of 2017. The metaphor of an ecumenical winter perhaps

---

166. See, concretely, the underappreciated proposal: Roman Catholic/Lutheran Joint Commission, "Facing Unity," in *Growth in Agreement II: Reports and Agreed Statements of Ecumenical Conversations on a World Level, 1982–1998*, ed. Jeffrey Gros, Harding Meyer, and William G. Rusch (Geneva: WCC, 2000) 443–84.

167. See the survey of this progress in Walter Kasper, *Harvesting the Fruits: Basic Aspects of Christian Faith in Ecumenical Dialogue* (New York: Continuum, 2009).

encourages the sense that a bit more effort will make the difference. After all, one season is always followed by the next. Will the present ecumenical winter be followed just as inevitably by a new ecumenical spring? Perhaps all that is needed is a bit of a nudge, a push for some dramatic ecumenical breakthrough during the 2017 commemoration that will renew possibilities that now seem close but unattainable.

Are such expectations setting us up for new disappointments? Much depends on how one reads the present ecumenical moment. Are we in a pause, awaiting the impending return of progress? Or have conditions changed in a more fundamental way.

We should use the present moment and the 2017 commemoration to reflect on the nature of ecumenical change. A clearer picture of ecumenical change can help us both grasp our own situation and understand what can be expected of the future.

How do large networks or structures, such as the network of Christian churches in their complex interactions, change? A major shift in the wider patterns of thought of the late twentieth century was a turn from an emphasis on gradual change along a somewhat predictable continuum to a new recognition of the way sudden and unpredictable change punctuates long periods of relative stasis. The fountainhead of this new approach was Thomas Kuhn's *The Structure of Scientific Revolutions*.[168] Kuhn argued that science is not the steady accumulation of data and analysis, producing a gradual growth in knowledge and understanding. Rather, the history of science needs to distinguish long periods of normal science, governed by a relatively stable set of assumptions and practices, and brief periods of revolutionary science, when basic assumptions are called into question; basic terms, such as matter or energy or elements, are redefined; and the sense of what is an interesting problem and how it should be addressed changes. These periods of revolutionary science lead to "paradigm shifts," a term Kuhn used in a much more precise sense than is usual today. Examples would be the shift into a modern understanding of chemical elements or the shift from Newtonian to relativistic and quantum-based physics. Such paradigm shifts are not just the accumulation of small changes. They often involve a redefinition of terms, making comparisons between statements made before and after the shift complicated. When such a revolution will occur and what shape it will take, how it will redefine what is considered conceptually possible and interesting, are unpredictable.

168. Thomas S. Kuhn, *The Structure of Scientific Revolutions*, 2nd ed. (Chicago: University of Chicago Press, 1970).

Developments and discussions of Kuhn's views have shown that revolutions do not mean utter discontinuity. While overarching understandings and the meanings of terms can shift, there is, Kuhn noted, the preservation of problems solved.[169] What is achieved in one period of normal science is not necessarily lost in the revolution that leads to another period of normal science. Especially when a "principle of interpretive charity" is at work, true sentences of one period are subsumed into new ways of speaking.[170]

A second example of such a shift from gradualism to some version of punctuational change is the macroevolutionary theory of punctuated equilibrium put forward by Niles Eldredge and Stephen Jay Gould.[171] Evolution at the expanded level of geologically measured time is not a slow and even, gradual process, but is dominated by stasis, punctuated by the comparatively rapid appearance of a new species. After its appearance, a species tends to be highly stable for long periods of time. Evolution is stepwise, not along a smooth incline.

A related concept is that the plant and animal life of a region typically exists in "coordinated stasis,"[172] a situation in which little change occurs in the species present until a "turn-over pulse" takes place, a relatively rapid group of extinctions and the development of new species. Stable patterns tend to hold until disruption forces a period of readjustment, leading to a new stable pattern. As Gould emphasized at the level of the species, stasis is not a passive and accidental by-product, but is actively maintained.[173]

A significant difference separates the history of science from the evolution of plants and animals. The history of science, and of human culture in general, is "Lamarckian," that is, what is learned in one generation is passed on to the next, rather than Darwinian, in which acquired characteristics are not inherited. As a result, cultural change can be more progressive.[174]

---

169. Ibid., 170. On the question of continuity across revolutions, see also Peter Godfrey-Smith, *Theory and Reality: An Introduction to the Philosophy of Science* (Chicago: University of Chicago Press, 2003) 94–98.

170. See here the subtle but difficult discussion in Donald Davidson, "On the Very Idea of a Conceptual Scheme," in *Inquiries into Truth and Interpretation* (Oxford: Oxford University Press, 1984) 196–97.

171. Stephen Jay Gould, *Punctuated Equilibrium* (Cambridge: Harvard University Press, 2007). Gould notes (283) that he was opened to ideas of less gradual and more punctuated change by reading Kuhn.

172. Carlton E. Brett, Linda C. Ivany, and Kenneth M. Schopf, "Coordinated Stasis: An Overview," *Palaeogeography, Palaeoclimatology, Palaeoecology* 127 (1996) 1–20.

173. Gould, *Punctuated Equilibrium*, 273.

174. Ibid., 267, 278.

The punctuated character of cultural change does not thus disappear. As progress is made under a paradigm, so also problems accumulate, contributing to the pressure toward a rethinking of basic notions.[175]

The temptation should be resisted to generalize rapidly and universally from these theories of change. Nevertheless, some patterns emerge:

- large-scale change in basic forms of thought and practice is not gradual, but tends to come in specific "revolutions" or "punctuations"

- the time between such punctuations is not changeless, but actively preserves a coordinated stasis, an interlocking system of identities and practices that preserves the basic pattern

- large-scale change is unpredictable, both in when it will occur and the shape it will take

- relative stasis is the normal state of affairs

- work for incremental change during periods of relative stasis can prepare for revolutions and punctuations, but the helpfulness of such incremental changes is unpredictable

Space does not here permit the development of a full theory of normal ecumenism, but the interrelations of churches do seem to follow a pattern of punctuational change. After centuries of relative stasis in interchurch relations, the twentieth century was a period of revolutionary ecumenical change: the creation of the World Council of Churches; the declaration on ecumenism of the Second Vatican Council; the lifting of the anathemas of 1054 by the pope and the ecumenical patriarch; agreements on Christology by the Catholic Church, the Orthodox Church, and the Oriental Orthodox churches; the *Joint Declaration on the Doctrine of Justification*; the virtual disappearance of serious doctrinal argument among mainstream Protestant denominations; and the rise of Pentecostal churches. Attitudes and behaviors have radically altered. The patterns of interchurch relations in place since the confessionalization period of the late sixteenth century have been broken up.

My suggestion is that for some time, this revolution has been slowing down, settling into a new set pattern. Achievements are being solidified, fruits harvested (to use the language of Cardinal Kasper's survey of Catholic-Protestant dialogues). The end of the revolution is not just a matter of fatigue, but of some problems proving insoluble, at least on the basis of

---

175. Kuhn, *Structure of Scientific Revolutions*, 66–76.

present terms of analysis and present forms of ecclesiastical life. As Cardinal Kasper's survey shows, while progress has been real and decisive on questions that are broadly soteriological—those addressing salvation and how it is received—progress has proved elusive on ecclesiological issues, addressing how the Church lives its life. In addition, new problems and disagreements have arisen, many related to deep ethical differences among the churches that cannot be resolved by the historical and conceptual methods developed in the ecumenical dialogues.

To use the language of Kuhn, we are at the end of a period of revolutionary ecumenism and entering a period of "normal ecumenism." Normal ecumenism would be a new pattern of interchurch relations which is neither the confessional antagonism of the late sixteenth to nineteenth centuries, nor the ecumenical revolution of the twentieth. It is not a return to the *status quo ante oecumenismo*, a loss of what has been achieved. Too much has changed and is now embodied in new behaviors and institutions. Nor is such a normal ecumenism a matter of dramatic breakthroughs. Breakthroughs may occur, of course. The theological differences between the Orthodox and Catholic churches seem to me surmountable and even the ecclesiological issues between them could, with sufficient good will, be overcome (although the internal institutional and social dynamics of the two churches may present decisive obstacles for the coming decades). Nevertheless, most of the breakthroughs that can be made within the constraints of present conceptual and social realities would seem to have been made.

If I am right and we are entering a period of normal ecumenism, then the ecumenical challenge for 2017 and the commemoration of the Reformation lies in the question of the churches' capacity to utilize the event as a platform for the exercise of such a new form of ecumenism. Can forms be found to commemorate the event in a way that encourages the continued recognition of commonalities despite differences? Can an openness to a true ecumenical exchange of gifts be maintained, rather than either a harmless but unengaged mouthing of platitudes or a retreat into confessional ghettos? Can the churches engage their differences in ways that are fruitful, even if the discussion makes clear just how intractable the differences are?

Ecumenical work is still to be done, but it needs to be attentive to the conditions within which it works.

Appendix: Some Resources and Other Information for Remembering 1517 and the Beginnings of the Reformation

Ecumenical Resources

Lutheran-Roman Catholic Commission on Unity. *From Conflict to Communion: Lutheran-Catholic Common Commemoration of the Reformation in 2017*. Leipzig: Evangelische Verlagsanstalt, 2013.

A text from the international Catholic-Lutheran dialogue meant to be a help to thinking about 2017. Might, however, be a bit academic for parish use, although that depends on the parish. Can be downloaded for free from various sites: put the title into a search engine to find them.

Study Guide: From Conflict to Communion

A parish resource, to be used along with the dialogue statement in educational settings—summaries, discussion questions, etc. It is extensive (forty-six pages) and may make the statement more user-friendly. Again, put the title into a search engine and you should find it.

Koch, Kurt. "'From Conflict to Communion': Principles and Possibilities for the Ongoing Ecumenical Process." Geneva, Switzerland, 2013. http://www.vatican.va/roman_curia/pontifical_ councils/chrstuni/ lutheran-fed docs/rc_pc_chrstuni_doc_20130617_presentation-card-koch_en.html.

Statement from the President of the Vatican ecumenical office on the *Conflict to Communion* text.

The Lutheran World Federation and The Roman Catholic Church. *Joint Declaration on the Doctrine of Justification.*

Available various places online. Put title into search engine.

Resources on 2017

Eires, Carlos M. N. *Reformations: The Early Modern World*, 1450-1650. New Haven, CT: Yale University Press, 2016.

MacCulloch, Diarmaid. *The Reformation.* New York: Viking, 2003.

A good general history of the Reformation; long, but a good read. Rather weak on theology, but good on events and comprehensive in its coverage, including such places as Poland and Spain.

Hendrix, Scott H. *Martin Luther: A Very Short Introduction.* Oxford: Oxford University Press, 2010.

A good, short introduction to Luther, his life and theology. Up-to-date in its scholarship, straightforwardly written. Excellent bibliography for further reading.

Luther, Martin. *The Freedom of a Christian.* Translated by Mark D. Tranvik. Minneapolis: Fortress, 2008.

The best single piece to read by Luther, in a recent translation that aims at greater readability. A somewhat partisan introduction, however.

http://www.e-ccet.org/2015/03/1517-reformation-timeline/

A detailed timeline of the first years of the Reformation.

http://www.luther2017.de/en

The English version of the website of the official "Luther Decade" in Germany. The "decade" is an ambitious project of state governments, more oriented to tourism than theology, but basic information about Luther and the Reformation is present.

https://www.lutheranworld.org/reformation-2017

Resource page on the programs of the Lutheran World Federation related to 2017.

"Indulgences as Ecumenical Barometer: Penitence and Unity in the Christian Life." *Bulletin of the Centropro Um'one* (Rome) 39 (2011) 3–9. Online: http://www.prounione.urbe.it/pdf/f_prounione_bulletin_n79_spring201 1.pdf.

Made in the USA
Monee, IL
02 July 2021